ORACLE®

*Oracle Press*™

# Java WebSocket Programming

## About the Author

**Danny Coward** is a Chief Architect and Web Architect at Oracle. He is the Specification Lead for the Java API for WebSocket for Java EE and Java SE/JavaFX. Coward's work leading WebSockets at Oracle makes him the leading expert on Java WebSocket programming. Coward has specialized experience in all aspects of Java software—from Java ME to Java EE to the founding of the JavaFX technology.

## About the Technical Editor

**Dr. Santiago Pericas-Geertsen** is a Principal Member of Technical Staff in the Sun Glassfish organization at Oracle, and an architect and technical lead in the Avatar project. Santiago is a Specification Lead for JSR 339, JAX-RS 2.0. While at Sun Microsystems, Santiago was a technical lead for the Glassfish Mobility Platform, a developer and lead in the Fast Web Services project, and a participant and editor in World Wide Web Consortium (W3C) initiatives. He holds two US patents, 7647415 and 7716577. Santiago blogs from Java.net, tweets from @spericas, and has presented at numerous academic and industry-oriented conferences.

*Oracle Press*™

# Java WebSocket Programming

Danny Coward

New York  Chicago  San Francisco
Athens  London  Madrid  Mexico City
Milan  New Delhi  Singapore  Sydney  Toronto

**Cataloging-in-Publication Data is on file with the Library of Congress**

McGraw-Hill Education books are available at special quantity discounts to use as premiums and sales promotions, or for use in corporate training programs. To contact a representative, please visit the Contact Us pages at www.mhprofessional.com.

**Java WebSocket Programming**

1 2 3 4 5 6 7 8 9 0   QFR QFR   1 0 9 8 7 6 5 4 3

ISBN    978-0-07-182719-5
MHID       0-07-182719-6

| | | |
|---|---|---|
| **Sponsoring Editor** | **Technical Editor** | **Production Supervisor** |
| Brandi Shailer | Santiago Pericas-Geertsen | George Anderson |
| **Editorial Supervisor** | **Copy Editors** | **Composition** |
| Patty Mon | Emily Rader | Cenveo Publisher Services |
| **Project Manager** | Nancy Rapoport | **Illustration** |
| Harleen Chopra, | **Proofreader** | Cenveo Publisher Services |
| Cenveo® Publisher Services | Susie Elkind | **Art Director, Cover** |
| **Acquisitions Coordinator** | **Indexer** | Jeff Weeks |
| Amanda Russell | James Minkin | |

This book is dedicated to Bill, Jared, and Alex.

# Contents at a Glance

# Contents

# Acknowledgments

**M**any thanks to Santiago for his thoughtful review comments during the writing of this book and to Brandi Shailer and Amanda Russell at McGraw-Hill Education for keeping me on track.

# Introduction

The WebSocket protocol is a new networking protocol for web developers' burgeoning toolbox. Aside from its inclusion as a core technology in HTML5 and its rapid adoption by all the major browsers from desktop to tablets and smartphones, why would the web developer care about yet another web technology?

## The Long Poll

By 2000, most major corporations worldwide had some kind of web presence. In the developing world, the personal computer revolution resulted in most households having Internet access through at least one channel. Businesses were rapidly building their presences on the Internet as a means of showcasing their products and services, and as a growing channel through which to deliver them. The basic technologies of the Web, such as HTTP, HTML, and JavaScript, were powering a revolution in how people interacted with one other, with their schools, and with their places of work; how they planned vacations; and even how they bought groceries.

Web sites grew from static and colorless catalog-style first efforts as developers sought new ways to make the web sites more interactive. They looked to add life to their web sites by injecting interesting information to their viewer at appropriate times and updating the information on the page as necessary. But developers found limits to basic HTTP and markup technologies. Developers needed to update the stock quote, the latest bid, the current list of friends logged into the same site, the new reduced price, the game result, and the latest celebrity to fall from grace. And they needed to do it all without relying on continuous interaction from the user. They needed to initiate data updates from the web servers to keep the web site fresh, engaging, and interesting. They needed a visitor to their web site to be transformed into a viewer of their channel, and they needed visitors to do as little as possible to absorb the information that was pushed to them.

Over the next few years, developers looked to a variety of less-than-formal means to accomplish the task of updating all the current visitors to a web site with the latest information of a variety of kinds. The most obvious means was to have the browser poll the server for updates. Developers would embed a short snippet of JavaScript into the relevant web page to force the browser to refresh the whole page at a predefined interval. This method would refresh all the data, whether the data fetched needed a refresh or not. The latency of the network was apparent in this method, and so the user experience was not good, even apart from the problem of fetching unneeded data.

A slightly more sophisticated approach was to use the HTTP Keep Alive mechanism. In this approach, JavaScript code inside the web page would keep open a long-lived HTTP connection, like a never ending download, that would periodically update with new information. Large differences in how long browsers and servers would keep the connection open resulted in problems, and typically, the client's browser would need to continually reopen the connection, whether or not there was data to fetch from the server.

As developers approached these techniques, development frameworks such as Comet and AJAX grew to support them and encompass these basic techniques. To some extent, they could hide some of the deficiencies of these basic approaches. There were, however, two fundamental problems that even the best implementations could not overcome. First, HTTP is an expensive network protocol for sending simple information. Just to ask for a simple stock quote update, the context of the connection has to be recalled each time it is made: all the header information such as that which qualifies the client and server platform, the authentication properties, the descriptions of the payload, and so on. Second, and worse, the expensive connections were made whether the server had new information to convey or not.

## Enter WebSockets

In 2009, work started on a technology that would allow the client to establish a lightweight connection with the server that would allow bi-directional communication and a lightweight content model. Servers would be able to push data to their connected clients only when they needed to. Once the connection was established, client and server alike would have a way to send simple information without having to re-create the context of the connection each time a message was sent.

The days of needless updates were coming to an end.

To understand how wasteful of network resources polling approaches can be, consider an auction web site. Items are posted on the web site, and users can place bids on the item for a defined period of time, at the end of which, the item is sold to the highest bidder. Throughout the length of the auction, any user visiting the auction page is able to view the current bid and use that information to decide on a higher bid. Let's say that the site puts up a highly desirable item for auction—a slightly used iPod (it is, after all, 2003)—and the time period of the auction for this item is only one hour. Suppose that when a new bid is made for the iPod, the web site needs to convey only a short message with the new price and perhaps some accompanying information like the bidder's online name. Let's estimate that you can always fit that into 64 bytes. Let's say that given that all the users are logged in, there are some cookies that need to be conveyed in the HTTP request for new information. Together with the content type header, perhaps a couple of application-specific headers, the content length, the browser ID, and so on, let's estimate about 512 bytes for the header information. Now assume you have, on average, 100 users logged into this web site, and on average, a new bid is made every 30 seconds throughout the auction. And let's say that the frequency of bidding is not evenly distributed; at some points, bids may be a few seconds apart (close to the end) and at other times (at the beginning) the bids may be minutes apart. A bidder will always want the latest price information available, so it would be prudent to refresh the price every two seconds; otherwise, a bidder may become frustrated when a bid does not go through because another bid was made before the bidder got the update. Let's add up all the data sent in order to receive the updates:

**30 updates per minute for 60 minutes = 1800 updates.**

**Each update carries about 512 bytes in header information each way.**

**Total header information sent and received = 1800 x 512 bytes = 921,600 = 900KB.**

Now, we said that each of the updates would contain 64 bytes. And in this auction, we said that there were 120 bids. So the total update information = 120 x 64 bytes = 7.5KB.

So a rough efficiency ratio of (useful data) to (repeated data) is calculated at 7.5 / 900 = 0.8%.

Not a good score, and we won't even get into how this efficiency ratio decreases for longer auctions.

The goal of WebSockets is to dramatically increase this kind of network efficiency by sending contextual information only when setting up the connection, and once the connection is established, to allow either peer of the connection to send messages, even simultaneously, with a minimal amount of contextual information to identify the message.

In this way, web pages connected to web servers are able to receive updates only when the server decides they needed them, and when such updates are sent, it is not necessary to weigh down the message with a large payload of contextual information about the connection.

# Introduction to the WebSocket Protocol

The WebSocket protocol is network protocol that allows two connected peers full duplex messaging over a single TCP connection. A good analogy for WebSockets is a phone call. When making a phone call, you initiate the call by dialing a number. If the party you are trying to call accepts the call by picking up the receiver, the connection is established. While the connection is active, both parties can speak at the same time if they want to (although it's not recommended for a free flowing conversation!) and both parties can hear what is being said even as they are talking themselves. This is what is meant by full-duplex communication. The connection remains active, whether or not anyone is talking, until either one of the parties decides to hang up.

In the case of WebSockets, the connection is established by means of an HTTP interaction WebSocket endpoint. The initiator of the connection sends a specially formulated HTTP request containing the URL of the WebSocket endpoint with which it wants to connect. That starts the ball rolling and is called the *opening handshake*. If the server is willing to accept the connection, the server formulates a special HTTP response called the *opening handshake response* and sends it back to the client. Now, the TCP connection may be established, and WebSocket messaging back and forth can ensue. The connection remains active until either party decides to terminate the connection, or until something external brings down the connection—such as a timeout due to inactivity or a problem with the physical network.

WebSockets are primarily used as a communication mechanism between web applications residing on a web server and browser clients, although there is nothing specific in the protocol that requires this deployment setup. Equally, WebSocket connections could be established between any two peers on the network, not necessarily a browser and a web server. However, because of the technology's roots, the most immediate opportunity for WebSocket technology is to bring to life otherwise static web sites, and easily enhance web sites and web applications with live data and activity.

In this setup, the WebSockets residing in the browser are created using a JavaScript API that has been standardized by the W3C, called the JavaScript WebSocket API. The WebSocket residing in the web server hosting the web site may be written in any number of languages. The popularity of WebSocket has been so sudden that many different languages and web platforms have begun to embrace it. In particular, the Java platform has been quick to build in support for WebSocket. The primary focus of this book is to explore the facilities of this new Java API, although some of the examples will rely on code that uses the JavaScript API for WebSockets.

The Java WebSocket API is a core feature of the latest Java EE 7 platform and any web developer already familiar with the other Java and/or Java-based technologies for building web applications, such as Java Servlets, JSPs, JavaServer Faces, or any of the many relatives of those technologies, should become familiar with WebSocket in the Java platform and think about bringing a fresh and modern feel to existing or future web applications by incorporating this technology. With this book, you will learn how to write WebSocket applications. You will learn all the major facilities of the Java WebSocket API, including the various messaging modes at your disposal and configuration options for your WebSocket applications, along with where you can store application state, how to configure WebSockets so that they can only be accessed securely, and how to integrate WebSockets into Java EE applications. The things you learn in each chapter of the book are backed up by example applications that illustrate the technical facilities.

This book contains eight chapters.

# Chapter 1: Java WebSocket Fundamentals

In this chapter, you dive straight into your first WebSocket application, the Echo application. Though simple, this application and this first chapter introduce the main features of the Java WebSocket API, and in so doing, form the foundation for the rest of the chapters in the book.

## Chapter 2: Java WebSocket Lifecycle

The second chapter examines the lifecycle of a WebSocket endpoint, the central component that you create in a WebSocket application. This lifecycle defines the framework by which you can manage resources used by the WebSocket endpoint, and most importantly, defines how to intercept WebSocket messages. The lifecycle is illustrated using the Lifecycle application, which presents the user with a set of traffic signals that highlight the key stages in the lifetime of a WebSocket endpoint.

## Chapter 3: Basic Messaging

This chapter explores the fundamental aspects of sending and receiving messages in a web application, using a collaborative group drawing application as its example application. The example uses a Java application as a client, so this chapter also illustrates the use of the Java WebSocket API on the client side as well.

## Chapter 4: Configurations and Sessions

Chapter 4 shows two of the most important objects in the Java WebSocket API: the WebSocket session object, which represents a conversation with a WebSocket peer; and the endpoint configuration object, which holds the configuration information for an endpoint. These objects are put into play to illustrate their features in an online chat example application.

## Chapter 5: Advanced Messaging

This chapter makes a thorough examination of all the options available to developers for sending and receiving WebSocket messages. Building on Chapter 3, we take a look at advanced topics, such as message encoding and decoding strategies, and synchronous and asynchronous messaging modes. The example application in this chapter uses a user interface to illustrate the messaging options available in the API.

## Chapter 6: WebSocket Path Mapping

Covering the nine rules of path mapping, this chapter explores all the options available in the Java WebSocket API for publishing a WebSocket endpoint to a URI so that peers are able to connect to it. Using a simple stock portfolio application, the chapter shows techniques of exact path mapping, template mapping, and query strings, and discusses the kind of situations in which you might choose one technique over another.

# Chapter 7: Securing WebSocket Server Endpoints

In this chapter, you learn how to limit access to a WebSocket endpoint only to certain users of a web application, and you learn how you can ensure that communication between WebSocket endpoints remains private. We revisit the stock portfolio application, applying security techniques to secure and personalize the application.

# Chapter 8: WebSockets in the Java EE Platform

The last chapter starts an exploration of how to integrate WebSocket endpoints into a larger Java EE application. Providing ways to share application information between WebSocket endpoints and other Java web components, and with Enterprise JavaBeans, we rework the chat application of Chapter 4 to leverage Java Servlets and EJBs, the two key components of the Java EE platform.

# Intended Audience

This book is suitable for the following readers:

**Web developers who wish to enhance web applications with interactive features**

**Rich client application developers who wish to interact with a WebSocket server application**

**Java EE developers interested in developing applications for HTML5-enabled browsers**

The book assumes you have a working knowledge of the Java programming language, some experience with the Java SE platform, and some knowledge of the JavaScript programming language. Some experience with web application development is probably useful in addition, although not necessary.

# Retrieving the Sample Applications

All the sample application code can be downloaded from the Oracle Press web site at www.OraclePressBooks.com. The files are contained in a Zip file. Once you've downloaded the Zip file, you need to extract its contents. The samples run on the Glassfish 4.0 application server, which you can freely download from http://glassfish.java.net/, and can be built using the NetBeans IDE, which can be freely downloaded from http://netbeans.org/.

I hope this book inspires you to write applications no one has thought of yet!

# CHAPTER
## 1

## Java WebSocket
## Fundamentals

T his chapter introduces the Java WebSocket API and gives a high-level tour of its functions. The chapter will dive right into the sample application, an application whose server side simply echoes any messages sent to it by its client. We will use it to illustrate the major features of the Java WebSocket API. In so doing, this chapter will establish a foundation for the major features covered in the rest of the book. If you need a refresher on the main concepts of the WebSocket protocol, please take a look at the Introduction before reading on.

# Creating Your First WebSocket Application

Since the core of the WebSocket protocol is to enable messaging between two peers, we will start our examination of the Java WebSocket API with the simplest of examples: the EchoServer application.

The EchoServer application is a client/server application. Its client is a small snippet of JavaScript running in your web browser, and its server is a WebSocket endpoint written using the Java WebSocket API and deployed as part of a web application running on the application server. When the user loads the web page into the browser, on his or her command, the snippet of JavaScript code is executed. The first thing this code does is connect to the Java EchoServer WebSocket endpoint residing in the application server, and immediately thereafter sends it a message. The Java EchoServer endpoint running on the application server awaits incoming connections, and when it receives a message from one of its connected clients, it immediately replies with an acknowledgement.

We will use this application to illustrate the key aspects of the WebSocket endpoint we have created, that is, the EchoServer. Although this example is particularly simple, a solid understanding of how to create and deploy it will take us on a short tour of the key features of the Java WebSocket API. While we will not dwell on any of the key features in order to see the bigger picture in this first examination of the API, it will serve as a good foundation from which to explore the features in much more detail in later chapters of this book.

This sample is generally set up in two pieces—first, and most important, the Java EchoServer endpoint that we will write and deploy on the server, and second, the web page containing a JavaScript WebSocket client that will run in a browser. Figure 1-1 shows a general diagram of the setup the sample will create.

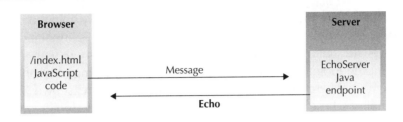

**FIGURE 1-1.**   *The Echo sample application*

# Creating a WebSocket Endpoint

Fortunately, creating your first WebSocket endpoint to put into a web application is very simple. All you have to do is write a Java class that implements the functionality you want the endpoint to have and understand how to apply to your class a small number of the Java annotations defined by the Java WebSocket API. For the EchoServer, we would like to implement the functionality that when it receives a message from a connected client it responds immediately with a message back to the client that sent the message.

So let's start by implementing that functionality right away. First, we'll create a Java class, called EchoServer, and add a method that takes a String parameter to hold any incoming messages as they arrive from the client. The return value of this method is also a String. We want the return value to be used to send a message back to the client whenever it sends an incoming one.

**Listing:**   *A Plain Old Java Object (POJO)*

```
public class EchoServer {
    public String echo(String incomingMessage) {
        return "I got this (" + incomingMessage + ")"
                        + " so I am sending it back !";
    }
}
```

At this point, you may be pleased to know that you have implemented all the logic this application will need! All that remains to do is use the Java WebSocket API to turn this plain old Java object into a WebSocket. To do this, we will need just two of the Java annotations from the Java WebSocket API: @ServerEndpoint and @OnMessage.

The `@ServerEndpoint` annotation is a class level annotation that is used to tell the Java platform that the class it decorates is actually going to be a WebSocket endpoint. The only mandatory parameter of this annotation is the relative URI (uniform resource identifier) that the developer wants to use to make this endpoint available under. This is a bit like giving someone the phone number where people are able to call them. In this case, we will keep things simple and use the URI /echo to publish this new endpoint we are creating.

So to the `EchoServer` class we add the following annotation:

**Listing:** *A POJO Evolving into a WebSocket Endpoint*

```
import javax.websocket.server.ServerEndpoint;

@ServerEndpoint("/echo")
public class EchoServer {
    public String echo(String incomingMessage) {
            return "I got this (" + incomingMessage + ")"
                                + " so I am sending it back !";
    }
}
```

You'll notice that the name of the attribute that defines the path under which the endpoint will be published is `value`, which means that you don't even need to put the name of the attribute in the annotation definition.

Now your code has enough information that the WebSocket implementation that will run it will know where in its URI space to publish it. You may be wondering to what URI the relative URI is relative: it's relative to the context root of the web application that will contain the EchoServer endpoint. We are not done turning this Java class into a WebSocket endpoint, however, because we have not yet told the implementation which of the methods we want it to call when it receives a message for this endpoint. It may seem obvious in this example, because your `EchoServer` class only has one method; but in a more complicated example, Java classes that are WebSocket endpoints may have several methods, some of which you may wish to be called when WebSocket events other than WebSocket messages occur, and some of which may not have anything directly to do with a WebSocket event. In any case, in order to mark your implementation method as being ready to handle any incoming messages, you use the method level `@OnMessage` annotation.

**Listing:** *A WebSocket Endpoint*

```
import javax.websocket.server.ServerEndpoint;
import javax.websocket.OnMessage;

@ServerEndpoint("/echo")
public class EchoServer {

    @OnMessage
    public String echo(String incomingMessage) {
            return "I got this (" + incomingMessage + ")"
                                + " so I am sending it back !";
    }
}
```

Believe it or not, you have just written your first WebSocket endpoint!

# Deploying the Endpoint

Deploying your EchoServer WebSocket endpoint is particularly simple. You need to compile the source file, include the class file in the WAR file, and deploy the WAR file. The web container will detect that there is a WebSocket endpoint included in the WAR file and do the necessary setup to deploy it. Once you have completed these steps, you are ready to make your first call to the WebSocket endpoint. We will see shortly for some other endpoints that there can be more setup to do in order to deploy them, but for now we can take a look at the client code that will call the endpoint we just created.

# Creating a WebSocket Client

In this and many of the examples in this book, the clients we will use to call the server endpoints that we develop will come in the form of snippets of JavaScript code utilizing the JavaScript WebSocket API. These snippets will be embedded in web pages that are bundled in the WAR file containing your WebSocket endpoints. The Java WebSocket API features a client API where, instead of using JavaScript in a web page to connect to a WebSocket server endpoint, developers can use the Java WebSocket API to create the client side of the application. We will see a Java client WebSocket application in Chapter 3. This and several of the other samples in the book, however, will make use of the simple JavaScript API because it is such a widespread choice in that it is supported in all browsers that support WebSockets.

In this sample application, the web client is a web page with a button that, when pressed, causes the WebSocket client to create a WebSocket connection to our EchoServer endpoint and send it a message. Whenever the JavaScript WebSocket receives a message, it displays it on the web page for you to see and closes the connection. We will see longer-lived WebSocket connections later in the book, but for now we are illustrating the first interactions very simply.

Here is a listing of the web page that will call the EchoServer, including most importantly the JavaScript WebSocket client code.

**Listing:** *An Echo JavaScript Client*

```html
<!DOCTYPE html>
<html>
    <head>
        <meta http-equiv="Content-Type" content="text/html; charset=UTF-8">
        <title>Web Socket JavaScript Echo Client</title>
        <script language="javascript" type="text/javascript">
            var echo_websocket;

            function init() {
                output = document.getElementById("output");
            }

            function send_echo() {
                var wsUri = "ws://localhost:8080/echoserver/echo";
                writeToScreen("Connecting to " + wsUri);
                echo_websocket = new WebSocket(wsUri);
                echo_websocket.onopen = function (evt) {
                    writeToScreen("Connected !");
                    doSend(textID.value);
                };
                echo_websocket.onmessage = function (evt) {
                    writeToScreen("Received message: " + evt.data);
                    echo_websocket.close();
                };
                echo_websocket.onerror = function (evt) {
                    writeToScreen('<span style="color: red;">ERROR:</span> '
                                                        + evt.data);
                    echo_websocket.close();
                };
            }

            function doSend(message) {
                echo_websocket.send(message);
                writeToScreen("Sent message: " + message);
            }

            function writeToScreen(message) {
                var pre = document.createElement("p");
                pre.style.wordWrap = "break-word";
                pre.innerHTML = message;
                output.appendChild(pre);
            }
```

```
        window.addEventListener("load", init, false);

    </script>
</head>
<body>
    <h1>Echo Server</h1>

    <div style="text-align: left;">
        <form action="">
            <input onclick="send_echo()" value="Press to send"
                                              type="button">
            <input id="textID" name="message" value="Hello Web Sockets"
                                              type="text">

            <br>
        </form>
    </div>
    <div id="output"></div>
</body>
</html>
```

Now if you run the application, you should get output shown in Figure 1-2.

**FIGURE 1-2.** *Echo sample output*

Now that you have created, deployed, and run your first WebSocket application, we can take a break from the code and turn to looking at this very simple application in terms of the fundamental Java WebSocket API concepts that it contains.

# WebSocket Endpoints

We use the term "endpoint" to mean one end of the WebSocket conversation. When you annotated the `EchoServer` class with the `@ServerEndpoint` annotation, it turned a plain old Java class into a logical WebSocket endpoint. When you deployed the application containing the `EchoServer` class, the WebSocket implementation made a scan of the WAR file that contains the `EchoServer` class and found that there was a WebSocket endpoint in it. Then it registered the class as a WebSocket endpoint so that when a client attempted to make a connection to the endpoint at the `/echo` URI, the WebSocket implementation created a new instance of the `EchoServer` class because the URI matched the one being requested and put that instance of the `EchoServer` class into service for the subsequent WebSocket conversation. This is the instance that was called when you pressed the button in the sample web page, and it lives as long as the WebSocket connection is active.

**NOTE**
*The endpoint is the central component model of the Java WebSocket API: every WebSocket application you create that uses the Java WebSocket API will have WebSocket endpoints in it.*

We have seen one of two ways in which you can use the Java WebSocket API to create endpoints. The EchoServer example showed you how you can use the annotations in the Java WebSocket API to turn a plain Java class into a WebSocket endpoint. The second way is to subclass the abstract `Endpoint` class included in the Java WebSocket API. If you do this, your subclass becomes a WebSocket endpoint, as we shall see in a moment.

**NOTE**
*There are two kinds of Java WebSocket endpoints: annotated endpoints and programmatic endpoints. Annotated endpoints are Java classes that have been transformed into Java WebSocket endpoints using Java annotations from the Java WebSocket API. Programmatic endpoints are Java classes that subclass the* Endpoint *class from the Java WebSocket API.*

Before discussing the circumstances under which you might want to choose to write annotated endpoints and the circumstances under which you might want to choose to write programmatic endpoints, you should know that, whichever approach you take, by and large you have access to most all of the features of the Java WebSocket API.

# Programmatic Endpoints

Since we have already taken a look at an annotated endpoint, let's take a look at a programmatic endpoint. The next example will soon become very familiar because you have seen it already: it is the same EchoServer sample as before, but written with a programmatic endpoint instead of an annotated endpoint.

In order to create the EchoServer server-side endpoint as a programmatic endpoint, the first thing we will do is write a Java class that subclasses the Endpoint class from the Java WebSocket API. In order to do so, the Endpoint class requires you to implement its onOpen() method. The purpose of this method is to breathe life into the instance of the endpoint that gets created as soon as a client connects to it. The parameters passed into this method are central classes in the Java WebSocket API. Before we get into any more details about the API, let's take a look at the code.

We will not list it here, but if you examine the JavaScript client to the programmatic EchoServer application, you will see that it is almost exactly the same as for the annotated EchoServer. The one difference is that it uses a different URI to connect to the programmatic EchoServer endpoint:

```
ws://localhost:8080/programmaticechoserver/programmaticecho
```

because the programmatic endpoint on the server is mapped to /programmaticecho instead of /echo, as we are about to see.

Now that we have that out of the way, let's look at the programmatic endpoint.

**Listing:** *A Programmatic Endpoint*

```
import java.io.IOException;
import javax.websocket.Endpoint;
import javax.websocket.EndpointConfig;
import javax.websocket.MessageHandler;
import javax.websocket.Session;

public class ProgrammaticEchoServer extends Endpoint {

    @Override
    public void onOpen(Session session, EndpointConfig endpointConfig) {
        final Session mySession = session;
        mySession.addMessageHandler(new MessageHandler.Whole<String>() {
            @Override
            public void onMessage(String text) {
                try {
                    mySession.getBasicRemote().sendText("I got this ("
                            +text + ") so I am sending it back !");
                } catch (IOException ioe) {
                    System.out.println("oh dear, something went wrong
                        trying to send the message back: " + ioe.getMessage());
                }
            }
        });
    }

}
```

The first thing to notice about the programmatic endpoint is that it is much longer than the annotated endpoint! For some people, this means they will usually choose to create annotated endpoints, but other developers are more familiar with the programmatic approach in general. Whichever approach you think you might end up preferring, this example is very useful to follow at this point, even if it seems more complicated than the annotated version, because even such a simple example brings us into close contact with some of the key objects in the API. The two objects passed into the mandatory onOpen() method are the Session and the EndpointConfig objects. These are very important objects to understand, even if you always choose the annotated approach over the programmatic approach when you create WebSocket applications, because you will need them over and over again.

# Fundamental Java WebSocket API Objects

The `Session` object in the Java WebSocket API gives the developer a view onto the open WebSocket connection. Each client connection to the ProgrammaticEchoServer endpoint is represented by a unique instance of the `Session` interface. It holds the means by which to adjust some of the properties of the connection; and, probably most importantly, it provides the endpoint a way to gain access to the `RemoteEndpoint` object. The `RemoteEndpoint` object represents the other end of the WebSocket conversation, and in particular provides the means by which the developer can send messages back to the client.

The other parameter of the `onOpen()` method is the `EndpointConfig` object. The `EndpointConfig` interface represents the information that the WebSocket implementation used to configure the endpoint. We will not discuss this interface much at this stage, as our example does not use it. For those readers who cannot wait, the API endpoint configuration is covered in some detail in Chapter 4.

Returning to the example, the first thing the implementation of the `onOpen()` method does is add a `MessageHandler` to the session. The `MessageHandler` interface (and its descendants) defines all the ways in which a programmatic endpoint can register its interest in receiving incoming messages. For example, developers can use `MessageHandler` interfaces to elect to receive text messages or binary messages, and they can elect to receive each message in one piece or, as is especially useful for developers of applications that exchange very large messages, in smaller pieces as the message arrives. In this example, we have implemented the most straightforward of the `MessageHandler` interfaces: the `MessageHandler.Whole<String>` interface. This interface defines how to register an interest in receiving text messages in one piece. It requires the developer to implement a single method, which is called by the WebSocket implementation every time a text WebSocket message arrives from the client:

```
public void onMessage(String text)
```

In the example, when the WebSocket implementation delivers such a text message, we immediately obtain a reference to the `RemoteEndpoint` that we are going to use to return a message right back to the client by calling the following method on the `Session` object:

```
public RemoteEndpoint.Basic getBasicRemote()
```

It is worth noting that there are two kinds of `RemoteEndpoint`: `RemoteEndpoint.Basic` and `RemoteEndpoint.Async`. Each subinterface of `RemoteEndpoint` provides a different way to send messages to the client it represents. The `RemoteEndpoint.Async` interface provides a number of methods for sending messages asynchronously; that is to say, its methods initiate the sending of a message but do not wait for the message to be sent before returning. This way, developers can be busy doing other work in their applications without the current working thread blocking until the message has actually been sent. The simpler `RemoteEndpont.Basic` interface defines a number of methods for sending messages to the client synchronously; that is to say, each `send` method call returns only when the message has been sent. In the example, this simpler approach is the one we have chosen to use. The call:

```
public void sendText(String text) throws IOException
```

on `RemoteEndpoint` sends the text message to the client, and you will see that it requires the developer to handle the checked `IOException`, which may be thrown if there is a problem with the underlying connection while sending the message.

Now that we have looked through the code, what happens when the programmatic endpoint is deployed is that when the client connects to the endpoint, the WebSocket implementation calls the `onOpen()` method on the `ProgrammaticEchoServer` class that we have just walked through. The `onOpen()` implementation creates the implementation of `MessageHandler` that is going to bounce back any text messages it handles to the client, and adds that `MessageHandler` instance to the session representing the client connection. Once that has been done, the method completes, and next time a text message arrives from the client on the connection, it will be routed by the WebSocket implementation to this `MessageHandler`'s `onMessage()` method.

Everything is exactly analogous to the annotated endpoint example. Or is it? The one missing piece that the programmatic endpoint does not have is the path to which we want to deploy the endpoint on the server. You will remember in the annotated endpoint example that the path was an attribute on the `@ServerEndpoint` example. In this programmatic endpoint case, assigning the path is a little more complicated. In order to deploy this example, we are going to have to tell the WebSocket implementation how to deploy the endpoint. In order to do that, we need to provide an implementation of the `ServerApplicationConfig` interface, which will provide this missing piece of information that the WebSocket implementation needs to deploy it.

The `ServerApplicationConfig` interface defines two methods that allow the developer to configure the endpoints in the application. Let's deal with the first method, because it is particularly simple:

```
public Set<Class<?>> getAnnotatedEndpointClasses(Set<Class<?>> scanned)
```

This method is called by the WebSocket implementation while it is deploying the application. The scanned parameter it passes is a `Set`, which contains all the Java classes that are annotated with the `@ServerEndpoint` annotation. In other words, it passes in all the annotated endpoints. The developer implements this method in such a way that it returns the `Set` of all the annotated endpoints he actually wants to be deployed. In general, returning the scanned set will allow the implementation to deploy all of the annotated endpoints in the WAR file. For example, in our application, there are no annotated endpoints, so the scanned set passed in will be empty.

The second method of the `ServerApplicationConfig` interface is the one we need to implement in order to deploy our programmatic endpoint:

```
public Set<ServerEndpointConfig>
    getEndpointConfigs(Set<Class<? extends Endpoint>> endpointClasses)
```

Like the method for annotated endpoints, this method is called during the application deployment phase. The `Set` passed into the method is the set of all classes that extend `Endpoint` in the application. That is to say, it is the set of all programmatic endpoints in the application. The developer has to implement this method so that it returns the set of `ServerEndpointConfig` objects that correspond to all the programmatic endpoints he or she wishes the WebSocket implementation to deploy. So in our case, the method is going to be called with one class in the `Set` passed in: the class is of course the `ProgrammaticEchoServer` class. What we need to do is create a `ServerEndpointConfig` object to return from the method that the WebSocket implementation will use to deploy the endpoint. Let's look at the code.

**Listing:**   *A ServerApplicationConfig for the Echo Sample*

```
import java.util.HashSet;
import java.util.Set;
import javax.websocket.Endpoint;
```

```
import javax.websocket.server.ServerApplicationConfiguration;
import javax.websocket.server.ServerEndpointConfiguration;
import javax.websocket.server.ServerEndpointConfigurationBuilder;

public class ProgrammaticEchoServerAppConfig
    implements ServerApplicationConfiguration {

    @Override
    public Set<ServerEndpointConfiguration>
      getEndpointConfigurations(Set<Class<? extends Endpoint>> endpointClasses

        ) {
        Set configs = new HashSet<ServerEndpointConfiguration>();
        ServerEndpointConfiguration sec =
          ServerEndpointConfigurationBuilder.create(
            ProgrammaticEchoServer.class,
            "/programmaticecho")
          .build();
        configs.add(sec);
        return configs;
    }

    @Override
    public Set<Class<?>> getAnnotatedEndpointClasses(Set<Class<?>> scanned){
        return scanned;
    }
}
```

You will see that from the getAnnotatedEndpointClasses() method we simply return the scanned set, which in this example is empty since there are no annotated endpoints in the WAR file containing this example. For the getEndpointConfigurations() call, we create a single endpoint configuration object that holds the path to which we want to deploy it and the class of our endpoint. Then we add it to the set of all endpoint configurations we want to deploy for this application and return it, which is an instruction to the WebSocket implementation to deploy this single programmatic endpoint to the given path /programmaticecho.

Then we deploy the WAR file to the application server in the same way as we did for the annotated endpoint example, and we get a similar result when we run the application.

This is additional evidence that, in some ways, choosing to create endpoints programmatically is more labor intensive! In the example, the programmatic endpoint itself has more code to do the same thing as the annotated endpoint. When you wanted to deploy the annotated endpoint, notice that you didn't have to give any more information or write any additional configuration code, whereas when you wanted to deploy the programmatic endpoint, you had to implement an interface in order to supply the configuration information.

To some extent, whether you will always want to stick to using annotated endpoints, programmatic endpoints, or a mixture of approaches, is a matter of personal taste. Some developers prefer the more traditional approach of using APIs explicitly. On the other hand, some developers prefer the brevity of the annotated style of programming and the additional flexibility it gives in being able to change configuration and setup information quickly by altering annotations rather than rewriting a configuration class. Functionally speaking, both approaches are largely equivalent, though there are cases where the programmatic approach gives greater control and more features that are not available through the annotated endpoint approach.

While this book leans toward the annotated approach, we will be sure to mix in examples of the programmatic approach as well. This book recommends that you learn the fundamentals of both approaches with an open mind in order to explore for yourself which approach will work best for the application (or applications) you are going to write, and what your own tastes will turn out to be.

# Inside the Echo Samples

Now that we have developed, deployed, and run our first applications, it's worth taking a moment or two to absorb what we have done by examining what is actually happening when we deploy and run our application. The simple functionality of these applications reveals some of the major elements of the Java WebSocket API. It is worth spending some time looking at these important building blocks because they will recur in some variant in nearly every WebSocket application you create.

## Deployment Phase

When we deploy the WAR file, which contains our endpoints to the application server, a number of things happen in order to ready the application for its first connection. The first is that the WebSocket implementation will examine the WAR file to try to locate any endpoints in it that may need to be deployed. First, the examination will locate any Java classes that are annotated with the `@ServerEndpoint` and any Java classes that extend the `Endpoint` class from the Java WebSocket API. It will also locate in the WAR file any classes that implement the `ServerApplicationConfig` interface; these classes will tell it how to deploy the endpoints.

Once the WebSocket implementation obtains this information, it uses it to build the set of endpoints to deploy. In the EchoServer sample, our WAR file simply held one annotated endpoint. If there are no `ServerApplicationConfig` implementations in the WAR file, the WebSocket implementation will automatically deploy all the annotated endpoints. This is indeed the case for our annotated endpoint example, so that is how that endpoint becomes deployed. In the programmatic Echo sample, the WAR file contains one implementation of the `ServerApplicationConfig` interface, so the WebSocket implementation instantiates this class once during the deployment phase and queries its methods to know which endpoints to deploy. In our programmatic endpoint example, the `ServerApplicationConfig` implementation asks that the single programmatic endpoint we wrote be deployed.

There are other deployment options for developers with the Java WebSocket API, and it is possible to package multiple `ServerApplicationConfig` implementations into the same WAR.

Once the implementation has determined the set of WebSocket endpoints to be deployed from the WAR file, most implementations will run other checks on the endpoints before proceeding any further and will only deploy an application that is well formed. Different WebSocket implementations may catch and report possible configuration or programming errors (such as two endpoints mapped to the same path or WebSocket annotations used at the wrong semantic level) at different points in the deployment phase and in different ways depending on how they are architected and designed. Some may report failures in a log file. Some that use tools with a graphical user interface may report helpful messages onscreen during the deployment of the application. However, if all is well and the application is valid, the WebSocket implementation will associate the endpoints with the URIs they declare, and then the application will be ready to accept incoming connections.

## Accepting the First Connection

You will remember from the Introduction that when initiating a WebSocket connection the first thing that has to occur is an initial HTTP request/response interaction. This interaction is called the *WebSocket opening handshake*. Many WebSocket developers will never need to understand the details of how this interaction works any more than you need to understand the mechanics of phone exchange or cellular networks to complete a phone call. We will, however, cover this topic in Chapter 4. Suffice it to say, at this point, that the client that wished to connect is armed with the full URI address, including the hostname and relative path from the hostname to where the endpoint is published, and it issues a specially formed HTTP request to that URI. There are other parameters that can be associated at this point with the client side of the opening handshake, and this is a topic we will return to in Chapter 4. When the server receives this opening handshake request, it examines the request and may perform a number of checks in the client. (For example, is the client issuing the request from where it said it came from? Is the client authorized to proceed?) If all is well, the server will return a specially formatted HTTP response, which will tell the client whether the server wishes to accept the incoming connection. In typical cases, all of this happens "under the covers" as far as the WebSocket developer is concerned, although in more advanced cases Java WebSocket developers may intercept this HTTP request and response interaction in order to customize it. We illustrate the concepts of the opening handshake in Figure 1-3.

If all is well formulated and there is indeed a WebSocket endpoint in the server registered to the address provided in the opening handshake, the connection is established. The WebSocket implementation will create a new instance of the endpoint, whether annotated or programmatic, that will be dedicated to interacting with that single client to which it is now connected. This means, for example, that if your WebSocket endpoint ends up with thousands of client connections to it, the WebSocket implementation will instantiate your endpoint thousands of times, one time for each new client that connects. Figure 1-4 shows an example of the opening handshake request.

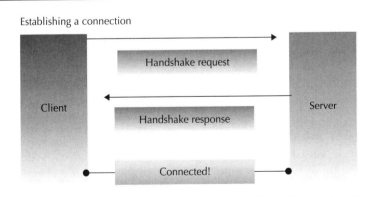

**FIGURE 1-3.**   *The opening handshake interaction*

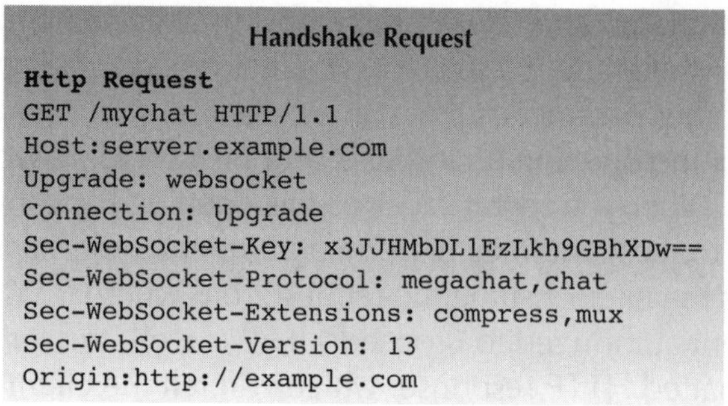

```
                    Handshake Request
Http Request
GET /mychat HTTP/1.1
Host:server.example.com
Upgrade: websocket
Connection: Upgrade
Sec-WebSocket-Key: x3JJHMbDL1EzLkh9GBhXDw==
Sec-WebSocket-Protocol: megachat,chat
Sec-WebSocket-Extensions: compress,mux
Sec-WebSocket-Version: 13
Origin:http://example.com
```

**FIGURE 1-4.** *An opening handshake request*

In this example, the client is requesting to connect to a WebSocket that is hosted by the server at `http://server.example.com` and whose URI relative to the root of the server is `/mychat`. You will notice that the WebSocket protocol uses the HTTP Upgrade mechanism, the same general mechanism that is used by browsers to upgrade an HTTP connection to a secure HTTPS connection, except that in this case the protocol the client is requesting is of course the WebSocket protocol. The client sends a unique token that will be used in the response, and you will notice that there are other headers defining the version of the WebSocket protocol the client wishes to use and that it wishes to use some particular subprotocols and extensions. We will touch on the exact definitions and uses of subprotocols and extensions of the WebSocket protocol in later chapters. At this point, simply know that they indicate ways in which a particular application can tune the protocol to better suit its needs.

Finally, the opening handshake request may also declare the `Origin` header, for example, if it is formulated by a browser, which is usually the Internet address of the web site that served the web page containing the WebSocket client code.

Figure 1-5 shows an example of an opening handshake response. In this example, the server has agreed to "upgrade" the connection to a WebSocket connection. It sends back a security token, which the client uses to verify that the response it received came in response to the same request it sent. The server in this example has decided to use the `chat` subprotocol of the list requested

```
                      Handshake Response

Http Response
HTTP/1.1 101 Switching Protocols
Upgrade: websocket
Connection: Upgrade
Sec-WebSocket-Accept: HSmrc0sMlYUkAGmm5OPpG2HaGWk=
Sec-WebSocket-Protocol: chat
Sec-WebSocket-Extensions: compress, mux
```

**FIGURE 1-5.**   *The opening handshake response*

in the opening handshake request. Since it supports both of the extensions
to the WebSocket protocol (called `compress` and `mux`—compression
and multiplexing, respectively), it has agreed to use those extensions in the
connection that has now been established between the client and server as
a result of this opening handshake.

# WebSocket Messaging

Now the Transmission Control Protocol (TCP) connection is established.
The WebSocket protocol defines a messaging protocol on top of TCP with
minimal framing. The different WebSocket protocol frames that are sent
backward and forward over the TCP connection define the lifecycle events
of the WebSocket, such as opening and closing the connection, while also
defining how application-created text and binary messages are transmitted
over the connection.

When the WebSocket implementation accepts an incoming connection, it
ensures that there is an instance of the endpoint that is able to handle it and
that it associates with the client making the connection. You will learn more
in the next chapter about the association between client connections and
endpoint instances. At this point, whenever the client sends a message to the
endpoint, it is the endpoint instance that the implementation has associated
with the client that receives the method callback with the message in the
payload. The endpoint may obtain a reference to a `RemoteEndpoint` object
through the `Session` object that uniquely represents the client to which
it is connected in order to send it a message. The same association exists
implicitly in the case of a return value from the message-handling method of

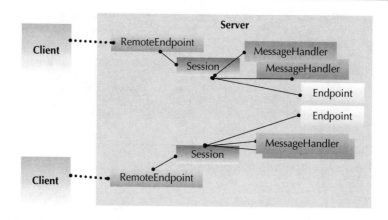

**FIGURE 1-6.** *An object snapshot of a Java WebSocket server application*

an annotated endpoint. Figure 1-6 shows a diagram of the object model that gets set up in the typical server deployment for programmatic endpoints.

In the diagram, we can see that deployed on the server we have a single logical endpoint, which has two instances represented by the two Endpoint boxes, each handling messages from two separate clients. Each instance of the endpoint has registered a number of MessageHandler instances to handle incoming messages. You can also see that each endpoint has a reference to the Session object representing the connection to each client. Each of those sessions references an instance of the RemoteEndpoint object, which gives the endpoint the ability to send messages back to the client.

For annotated endpoints, the object model set up at run time is largely the same, with the Session and RemoteEndpoint objects always available to the endpoint. There is one simplification, however, and that is that the MessageHandler objects for annotated endpoints are generated by the WebSocket implementation; the developer never has to create, register, or reference them.

Of course, this picture represents only a snapshot of the objects while the connection is active. As a complete picture of a WebSocket endpoint, it is only as complete as a single photograph of two people speaking on the phone is a complete description of a phone conversation. To more fully understand a complete WebSocket conversation between two endpoints, we need to delve into the WebSocket endpoint life cycle. This will be the topic of the next chapter.

# Summary

In this chapter, you have seen how to create a simple client/server WebSocket application that uses the Java WebSocket API to create the server element and the JavaScript API to create the client element. You have also seen how WebSocket endpoints can be created either by using Java annotations from the Java WebSocket API or programmatically by extending the `Endpoint` class in the Java WebSocket API. The chapter touched on some of the most important objects of the Java WebSocket API: the `Session`, `RemoteEndpoint`, and `MessageHandler` objects. It also examined two ways in which WebSocket endpoints are deployed as part of a standard web application.

# CHAPTER
## 2

## Java WebSocket Lifecycle

I n this chapter, we will examine the lifecycle of the WebSocket endpoint. The WebSocket endpoint lifecycle offers the developer a framework for managing resources needed by the endpoint, as well as a framework for intercepting messages. We will look closely at the sequencing and semantics of the lifecycle events and how the Java WebSocket API provides API and annotation support for processing them. We will see how they can be applied in a sample application in both annotated and programmatic form.

# The WebSocket Protocol

We'll start with a little background on the WebSocket protocol itself. Readers need not know every detail of this section in order to be able to use the Java WebSocket API, but it serves as a useful background to help in a general understanding of WebSocket technology and why the Java WebSocket API is the way it is.

Unlike HTTP-based technologies, the WebSockets have a lifecycle that is underpinned by the WebSocket protocol itself. For example, in servlet technology, the underlying protocol defines only a simple request/ response interaction that is wholly independent of the next interaction. In fact, in most cases the underlying network connection that carried it will vanish completely. Technologies such as the Java Servlet API have had to build conventions on top of this request/response interaction model to help developers create applications that live longer than the scope of single, isolated interactions: the `HttpSession` and the Java Servlet component lifecycle are good examples of this.

In contrast, the WebSocket protocol defines a longer-lived and dedicated TCP connection between a client and a server, and because it does so, it goes further in defining a longer lifecycle than the traditional web request/ response model. In addition, the WebSocket protocol defines the format of individual chunks of data that are transmitted backward and forward over the WebSocket connection. Once the connection has been established, these transmissions are framed with metadata that describes their purpose. There are two main types of frames in the WebSocket protocol: control frames and data frames. The control frames are transmissions of data that perform some housekeeping function of the protocol. For example, the protocol defines a close frame. The *close frame* is a particular transmission that means the sender is going to close down the connection. The other control frames are the ping and pong frames. *Ping and pong frames* are transmissions of data that serve as a check on the health of the connection: if a WebSocket wants to check up on the health of the connection it has with a WebSocket peer, it can send a ping frame. Upon receiving a ping frame, the WebSocket peer in turn must respond as soon as it can with a pong frame. Mimicking a game of ping/pong, the health of the connection (how fast it is, or whether it is functioning at all) can be checked at any time.

The other kind of frame defined by the WebSocket protocol is the data frame. A *data frame* defines the kind of WebSocket transmission that carries application data. The echo messages you sent in Chapter 1 are examples of text data frames. Data frames come in two basic types, textual and binary, one to carry text messages and one to carry binary data such as image data. One feature of the WebSocket protocol is that it is able to transmit messages, whether they are textual or binary, over multiple individual transmissions. Such an individual transmission that carries part of a complete message as part of a sequence of such transmissions is called a *partial frame.* This technique of sending a message as a sequence of partial frames is particularly useful when the WebSocket implementations are sending very large messages, or for sending messages even as they are being formulated. While the protocol is most often used for sending only short messages, there is no defined limit on the size of a WebSocket message, so there will be some applications that choose to use WebSocket messages to carry very large amounts of data, such as a video or a large archive of financial data.

As you will see, hints of the low-level WebSocket protocol framing are apparent in some of the Java WebSocket API calls, though developers really don't need to understand this lower level of detail.

# Lifecycle of a Java WebSocket

Now that you understand a little of what is going backward and forward over the wire during a WebSocket session, let's look at how the Java WebSocket API models the lifecycle of an endpoint.

The first event in the lifecycle of any Java WebSocket endpoint is the *open notification,* which is the indication that the connection to the other end of the WebSocket session has been established. Using an analogy to a phone call, in Chapter 1 we talked about the handshake interaction being akin to the kind of negotiation that happens during the establishment of an Internet telephone call: the routing of the number, the selection of the connection speed to use, and whether to use voice only or whether to use a video connection as well. Well, the open notification is analogous to the termination of the ring tone and the click establishing that the connection is now open.

Once the open notifications have been received by both ends of the WebSocket conversation, either participating WebSocket can then send a message. How many messages get sent, with what timing, in what order, and with what contents is, of course, very dependent on the application. In our analogy to a phone call, this is the time during the lifecycle when each party in the conversation takes the opportunity to say what they want to say during the call.

At any time during the WebSocket conversation, there may be some kind of error during transmission of a message. The WebSocket endpoint receiving the message may itself generate an error (for example, if it receives a message it does not know how to handle properly), or the WebSocket implementation itself may generate an error in response to some situation (for example, if it receives a message that is bigger than it is able to handle). This stage in the WebSocket endpoint lifecycle may result in one of two outcomes: either the error will be fatal, in which case the connection will be closed and no more messages will be able to be sent, or the error will be nonfatal and the endpoint will be able to continue sending and receiving messages if it wishes to. In the analogy of the phone call, messages may come in to either end of the conversation, which are garbled for a while but then become coherent again, or some more serious error may in fact cause the call to terminate.

When either party in the WebSocket conversation is ready to end the conversation, it can initiate a close event. In this case, the WebSocket implementation communicates to the other end of the conversation to notify it that the connection is about to close. In the analogy of the phone call, this is a little like the party in the call that is ready to end it by saying "goodbye" to terminate the call. Actually, the WebSocket protocol does not need to wait for the other end to acknowledge this notification, which is a little like hearing the phone click immediately after your conversation partner has said goodbye, but before you have a chance to respond in kind. A little rude, perhaps, for humans on a phone call, but perfectly adequate for WebSocket endpoints!

Let's review the lifecycle of a WebSocket conversation with the help of a diagram (see Figure 2-1). Here we can see by looking at the diagram from top to bottom that, once the WebSocket connection is established between the client and the server, each end of the WebSocket conversation is notified of the session opening. Once the session has been opened, each end of the WebSocket conversation receives a number of messages from the other party.

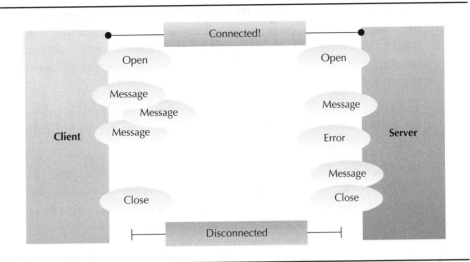

**FIGURE 2-1.** *WebSocket conversation lifecycle*

During this stage, some error condition may arise which, in the case of this diagram, is recoverable because the server endpoint that received the error gets delivery of another message after it has had a chance to process the error. In the diagram, one end of the WebSocket conversation has decided it wants to end the conversation, which causes each party to receive a close notification. No more messages can be sent now between the client and the server unless a new connection is established.

# The WebSocket Lifecycle in the Java WebSocket API

Now that we have looked at a basic description of the lifecycle of a WebSocket endpoint, let's take a look at how the lifecycle appears from the point of view of a Java component. In the previous section, we identified four events in the lifecycle of a WebSocket endpoint:

> **The open event** This is the event that occurs when a new connection is established with the endpoint and before any of the other events can happen.

**The message event**   This is the event of receiving a message from the other end of the WebSocket conversation. This can happen at any time after the WebSocket endpoint has received an open event and before the WebSocket endpoint has received a close event closing the connection.

**The error event**   This is the event generated when there is some error that has been raised on the WebSocket connection or by the endpoint.

**The close event**   This is the event that signifies that the connection the WebSocket endpoint is currently part of is about to close and can be initiated by either endpoint participating in the connection.

Fortunately, these events map pretty much one to one to methods that you can write to intercept these events on a Java component. First, let's take a look at the annotated WebSocket endpoint. Once we have done that, we will look at the same events as they show up on a programmatic endpoint.

# Annotated Endpoint Event Handling

To declare a Java class as a WebSocket endpoint, you use one of the class level annotations: @ServerEndpoint for server-side endpoints (which we saw in the first chapter), or the analogous @ClientEndpoint annotation for client endpoints (which we will see more of in Chapter 3). Let's assume for now that we are writing an endpoint that will be deployed on a server and will await incoming connections from one or more clients.

For annotated endpoints, in order to intercept the different lifecycle events, we make use of the method level annotations: @OnOpen, @OnMessage, @OnError, and @OnClose. We will see that each WebSocket lifecycle event is accompanied by different qualifying information. Therefore, there are a number of options for what the possible method signatures can be for Java methods annotated with the lifecycle annotations.

## @OnOpen

Let's start with the first one: @OnOpen. This annotation is used on a method of an annotated endpoint to indicate that it should be called when a new connection has been established to this endpoint. The main reason to have a method to handle the open event is so that you can do any kind of setup of information you might need during the WebSocket conversation. A good example of this might be that if your WebSocket is going to use a database to retrieve or store information from the WebSocket conversation, you would want to perform any expensive operations needed to prepare the database, such as opening a connection to it in the method that handled the open event. There are three pieces of information that accompany this event: the WebSocket `Session` object that represents the connection that has been established; the configuration object, an instance of `EndpointConfig` that contains the information that was used to configure the endpoint; and the set of path parameters that were found when the WebSocket endpoint was matched against the incoming URI during the opening handshake. One of the nice things about using the WebSocket annotations is that you don't have to use all the information about the event if you don't need to. So the kinds of methods for which you can use the `@OnOpen` annotation are any public methods with no return value that have an optional `Session` parameter, an optional `EndpointConfig` parameter, and any number of `String` parameters marked with the `@PathParam` annotation. In addition, the parameters you elect to include can appear in any order. We will return to the topic of path parameters in Chapter 6, so we will not spend much time on them here. This means that you could have the following if you just wanted a reference to the `Session` object:

**Listing:**  *Example Open Event Handling Method*

```
@OnOpen
public void init(Session session) {
      // initialization code
}
```

Additionally, if you wanted to query the configuration object (represented by an instance of the `EndpointConfig` class), you could equally declare the following:

**Listing:**  *Example Open Event Handling Method*

```
@OnOpen
public void init(Session session, EndpointConfig config) {
      // initialization code
}
```

You can already see that you have some flexibility, not just in naming your method to handle the open event, but also in how much of the data that accompanies the event you want to have available.

## @OnMessage

Typically, you will want your WebSocket endpoint to handle some or all of the incoming messages once the connection has been established. For this, we use the @OnMessage annotation. This allows you to decorate the method or methods that you would like to handle incoming messages. The information that accompanies the message event in the Java WebSocket API is the Session object, which represents the connection on which the message has arrived, the EndpointConfig, the path parameters that were found while matching the incoming URI during the opening handshake, and, most importantly, the message itself. As with the @OnOpen annotation, the method parameters may be listed in any order, and you only need to include method parameters for those parts of the message event you would like to know about.

The message will arrive on the connection in one of three basic forms: a text message, a binary message, or a pong message. The Java WebSocket API gives you a range of options for how you are able to receive messages of these shapes. The most basic forms you can elect to use are a String parameter if your method will handle text messages; a ByteBuffer or byte[] parameter if your method will handle binary messages; and an instance of the PongMessage interface, which is part of the Java WebSocket API, if your message will handle only pong messages.

For example, if you would like to handle text messages in the simplest form, you could have the following:

**Listing:** *Example Text Message Handling Method*

```
@OnMessage
public void handleTextMessages(String textMessage) {
     // process the textMessage here
}
```

If you would like to handle binary messages and also have a reference to the session representing the connection on which the message came, you could use the following:

**Listing:** *Example Binary Message Handling Method*

```
@OnMessage
public void processBinary(byte[] messageData, Session session) {
     // process binary data here
}
```

There are, however, a number of more advanced options for text and binary messages. For example, you can elect to receive text and binary messages in parts as they arrive. In this case, you use a pair of parameters to represent the arrival of a partial message: a `String` and `boolean` for partial text messages. The `String` represents the partial text message, and the `boolean` is a flag that is set to `false` if there are more partial messages in the sequence representing the whole text message to come or is set to `true` if the piece that is arriving is the last one in the sequence. For partial binary messages, you can choose a pair of either `ByteBuffer` and `boolean`, where the `ByteBuffer` represents the partial binary message and the `boolean` indicates whether the partial binary message that is arriving is the last one in the sequence of partial binary messages that forms the complete message. For binary messages, you can use the pair `byte[]` and `boolean`, which is the same as the `ByteBuffer` and `boolean` pair, except that it uses a byte array to hold the partial binary message instead of a `ByteBuffer`.

**Listing:**   *Example Partial Binary Message Handling Method*

```
@OnMessage
public void processVideoFragment(byte[] partialData, boolean isLast) {
     if (!isLast) {
          // there is more to come !
     } else {
          // now we have the whole message !
     }
}
```

**Listing:**   *Example Partial Text Message Handling Method*

```
@OnMessage
public void catchDocumentPart(String text, boolean isLast) {
     // pass on to feed elsewhere
}
```

Short messages of either type may still arrive in one piece if you use this partial message processing option. Longer messages may arrive in any number of pieces. In general, it is up to the implementation how it chooses to deliver messages to your API: different implementations may break messages into smaller pieces. However, in general, this is a useful option for handling large messages where you want to be able to start processing the message as soon as some of it arrives.

One more option you have for processing incoming messages using the `@OnMessage` annotation is to elect to process them using Java I/O streams—`java.ioReader` for text messages and `java.io.InputStream` for binary messages, which can be useful when trying to use one of the many Java libraries that uses I/O for processing the messages.

**Listing:**  *Example Binary I/O Message Handling Method*

```
@OnMessage
public void handleBinary(InputStream is) {
      // read
}
```

There are, in fact, still more options for handling messages: you can even have the WebSocket implementation translate the incoming message into an object of your own choosing. We will return to this topic in much more detail in Chapter 3.

WebSocket applications are generally asynchronous in their bidirectional messaging. That is to say, typical applications do not always respond immediately to an incoming message. There are, however, some cases where you do want to respond right away to an incoming message: the Echo sample applications in Chapter 1 are excellent examples of when you would want to do so. So there is one more option in the kind of method you can annotate with the `@OnMessage` annotation: you can have a return type or void. If you do have a return type on the method or methods you annotate with the `@OnMessage` annotation, the return value will be used by the WebSocket implementation to immediately return it as a message to the sender of the message you have just handled in your method. This is useful in particular cases where you may need to design an application that explicitly acknowledges receipt of a WebSocket message.

**Listing:**  *Example Message Handling Method with Return*

```
@OnMessage
public byte[] dealWithRequest(String requestMessage) {
      byte[] ack = {0};
      return ack;
}
```

In this example, when the endpoint that holds this method receives any kind of text message, the endpoint immediately returns a binary message containing the 0 byte as a payload. The most basic types you can return from a message annotated with the @OnMessage annotation are String and byte[] or ByteBuffer. There are more options, as you will see in the next chapter.

## @OnError

The error event is somewhat simpler than the message event. The @OnError annotation may be used to annotate a method on a WebSocket endpoint that will handle any errors that occur while the WebSocket implementation is processing incoming messages. Your WebSocket endpoints do not have to handle these kinds of errors if you do not want them to. However, it is advisable to include an error-handling method on your WebSocket endpoint; otherwise, you may end up wasting time trying to track down messages that do not get delivered to your endpoint from a client! The information that accompanies the error event is the error, the session on which the error occurred, and any path parameters associated with the opening handshake that established the connection. Again, we will return to the topic of path parameters in a later chapter. The error information is represented by the java.lang.Throwable class, and the session by the Session interface of the Java WebSocket API. As with the other method-level annotations of the Java WebSocket API, which of the parameters your error handling method includes depends on the information you would like to receive when the event occurs. As with the other method level annotations, the parameters you do choose to include may be listed in any order.

**Listing:** *Example Error Handling Method*

```
@OnError
public void errorHandler(Throwable t) {
        // log error here
}
```

There are three basic types of errors that can occur as a result of processing an incoming message. First, WebSocket implementation-generated errors can occur, for example, if an incoming message destined for the WebSocket endpoint is malformed. These errors are all of the type SessionException. Second, errors can occur when the WebSocket implementation tries to decode an incoming message into some object that the developer has asked for. We will come back to this topic in the Chapter 3, but for now, suffice it to say that errors of this kind are all `DecodeException` errors. Finally, runtime errors are generated by other methods of the WebSocket endpoint.

If you do not choose to include an error handling method in your application, the WebSocket implementation will log any errors generated during the operation of your WebSocket endpoint somewhere for you to look at later. Of course, it will depend on which WebSocket implementation you are using as to where you can find this information, and how detailed it is.

## @OnClose

We come now to the final event in the WebSocket's lifecycle, the close event. Intercepting the close event is a good idea if you have been using any expensive resources during the WebSocket conversation and want to release them and close them out properly. It is also good for other general cleanup when you know the WebSocket connection is closing. The `@OnClose` annotation can be used to annotate a number of different kinds of methods to handle the close event. The information that accompanies the close event is the session that is closing, any path parameters that were associated with the opening handshake that established the connection, and some information that describes the reason for the connection closing. This last information comes in the form of the `CloseReason` class in the Java WebSocket API. It holds both a code that defines the reason for the closure, together with a string message that may hold a message that describes further the reason for the closure. There are many reasons why the connection may be closed, but typically it is because either end of the WebSocket conversation decided it finished all it needed to do or because the connection timed out due to inactivity. As usual, the method parameters are optional and may appear in any order.

**Listing:**   *Example Close Event Handling Method*

```
@OnClose
public void goodbye(CloseReason cr) {
        // log the reason for posterity
        // close database connection
}
```

Now we will put all these ideas together in the form of a sample that illustrates the main concepts.

## Lifecycle Sample

The Lifecycle sample is a Javascript WebSocket client that talks back to a Java WebSocket endpoint that uses all the lifecycle annotations. When the `LifecycleEndpoint` annotated endpoint running on the server handles a WebSocket lifecycle event, it sends a message to the client that the client uses to display a set of traffic signals. When the application starts, the connection is closed. Pushing the buttons in the web page steps the user through the key stages in the WebSocket lifecycle, as you can see in the pictures shown in Figure 2-2. You will notice that there are two buttons that close the connection: one that causes the client to initiate the close and another that causes the server to initiate the close.

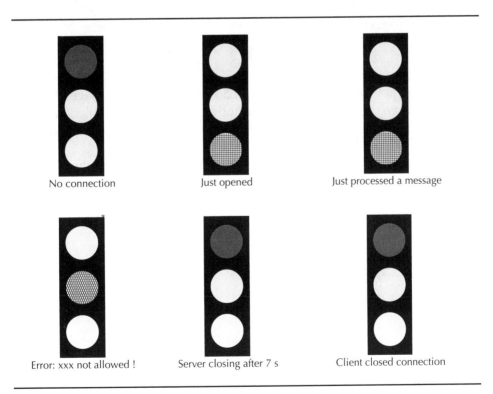

| No connection | Just opened | Just processed a message |
|---|---|---|

| Error: xxx not allowed ! | Server closing after 7 s | Client closed connection |
|---|---|---|

**FIGURE 2-2.** *Lifecycle traffic signals*

## Lifecycle JavaScript Client

The JavaScript code uses the JavaScript WebSocket API to intercept messages sent from the Java `LifecycleEndpoint` and parses the message that tells it which light to illuminate in the signal and what message to display to the user.

Let's first take a look at the JavaScript code, just focusing on the main client calls. As usual, we create the JavaScript WebSocket, adding event handling code that will be called whenever the server component sends back one of the messages that will instruct the client on how to display the traffic signals:

**Listing:** *Creating a JavaScript WebSocket*

```
function open_connection() {
        lifecycle_websocket =
            new WebSocket("ws://localhost:8080/lifecycle/lights");
        lifecycle_websocket.onmessage = function (evt) {
                update_for_message(evt.data);
                update_buttons();
        };
        lifecycle_websocket.onclose = function (evt) {
                update_buttons();
        };
}
```

As you can see, when the JavaScript WebSocket receives a message, it will call the `update_for_message()` method and update the enabled/disabled state of the buttons. Also, you can see that the same button update is called when the JavaScript WebSocket closes.

Next, we have two methods that will parse the message from the server. An example of one of those messages is "3:Just opened". The first method strips off the message part and returns the number; the second method strips off the number at the beginning and returns only the message part.

**Listing:** *JavaScript Parsing of the Lifecycle Messages*

```
function get_light_index(message) {
        return message.substring(0, 1)
}

function get_display_message(message) {
        return message.substring(2, message.length)
}
```

The next method calculates the color of each light in the traffic signal based on its position in the traffic signal (light _ index) and whether it should be switched on or off (light _ on _ index).

**Listing:** *JavaScript Calculating the Light Color*

```
function get_color(light_index, light_on_index) {
        if (light_index == 1 && light_on_index == 1) {
                return "red"
        } else if (light_index == 2 && light_on_index == 2) {
                return "yellow"
        } else if (light_index == 3 && light_on_index == 3) {
                return "green"
        } else {
                return "grey"
        }
}
```

Finally, here is the method that pulls everything together: it is called with parsed elements of the message sent by the server, and its purpose is to update the traffic signal and the message underneath it:

**Listing:** *JavaScript Updating the Page in Response to a Lifecycle Message*

```
function update_display(light_index, display_message) {
        var old = traffic_light_display.firstChild;
        var pre = document.createElement("pre");
        pre.style.wordWrap = "break-word";
        pre.innerHTML = "<b><font face='Arial'>"+display_message+"</font></b>";
        if (traffic_light_display.firstChild != null) {
                traffic_light_display.replaceChild(pre,
                                traffic_light_display.firstChild);
        } else {
                traffic_light_display.appendChild(pre)
        }
        var context = document.getElementById('myDrawing').getContext('2d');
        context.beginPath();
        context.fillStyle = "black"
        context.fillRect(65,0,70,210);
        context.fill();

        context.beginPath();
        context.fillStyle = get_color(1, light_index);
        context.arc(100,35,25,0,(2*Math.PI), false)
        context.fill();

        context.beginPath();
        context.fillStyle = get_color(2, light_index);
```

```
context.arc(100,105,25,0,(2*Math.PI), false)
context.fill();

context.beginPath();
context.fillStyle = get_color(3, light_index);
context.arc(100,175,25,0,(2*Math.PI), false)
context.fill();
}
```

We note that this example uses the new drawing canvas that is part of the same HTML5 specification that WebSockets is part of.

## Lifecycle Annotated Endpoint

Now that we've seen what the client of the application is doing, let's return to the topic of the WebSocket endpoint lifecycle. Let's take a look at the server component we created the Lifecycle annotated endpoint. Here is the complete listing:

**Listing:** *Lifecycle Java WebSocket Endpoint*

```java
import java.io.*;
import java.io.IOException;
import javax.websocket.OnClose;
import javax.websocket.OnError;
import javax.websocket.OnMessage;
import javax.websocket.OnOpen;
import javax.websocket.Session;
import javax.websocket.server.ServerEndpoint;


@ServerEndpoint("/lights")
public class LifecycleEndpoint {
    private static String START_TIME = "Start Time";
    private Session session;

    @OnOpen
    public void whenOpening(Session session) {
        this.session = session;
        session.getUserProperties().put(START_TIME,
                        System.currentTimeMillis());
        this.sendMessage("3:Just opened");
    }

    @OnMessage
    public void whenGettingAMessage(String message) {
        if (message.indexOf("xxx") != -1) {
            throw new IllegalArgumentException("xxx not allowed !");
        } else if (message.indexOf("close") != -1) {
            try {
```

```
                this.sendMessage("1:Server closing after "
                        + this.getConnectionSeconds() + " s");
                session.close();
            } catch (IOException ioe) {
                System.out.println("Error closing session "
                                        + ioe.getMessage());
            }
            return;
        }
        this.sendMessage("3:Just processed a message");
    }

    @OnError
    public void whenSomethingGoesWrong(Throwable t) {
        this.sendMessage("2:Error: " + t.getMessage());
    }

    @OnClose
    public void whenClosing() {
        System.out.println("Goodbye !");
    }

    void sendMessage(String message) {
        try {
            session.getBasicRemote().sendText(message);
        } catch (Throwable ioe) {
            System.out.println("Error sending message "
                                    + ioe.getMessage());
        }
    }

    int getConnectionSeconds() {
        long millis =  System.currentTimeMillis()
            - ((Long) this.session.getUserProperties().get(START_TIME));
        return (int) millis / 1000;
    }
}
```

First, we notice that this is a server endpoint using the `@ServerEndpoint` annotation, which is mapped to the path `/lights`. You may be wondering how to work out the full URI to the endpoint without of course looking at the client code that needs it to initiate the connection. The full URI is the `ws://` URI formed with the hostname and port number, plus the context path of the web application containing the WebSocket endpoint, plus the relative URI of the endpoint. We will come back to this in Chapter 6, but this means that since the context path of the web application containing the Lifecycle endpoint is `/lifecycle`, the complete URL to the WebSocket endpoint is

```
ws://localhost:8080/lifecycle/lights
```

You will see in the example that the method that has been designated with the @OnOpen annotation to handle the open event for this WebSocket endpoint is the following method:

**Listing:** *Lifecycle Open Event Handling Method Signature*

```
@OnOpen
public void whenOpening(Session session)
```

We have opted to receive the reference to the `Session` object, which we keep around for later use. By looking at the implementation of this method, we see that what we are doing in this endpoint in response to receiving the open event is noting the current time, adding it to the dictionary of user properties on the `Session` object, and then sending a message to the client indicating that we want the third (green) light to be switched on to indicate that message traffic may now flow.

You will also see in the example that we have indicated that the following method should be called whenever a message is received:

**Listing:** *Lifecycle Message Event Handling Method Signature*

```
@OnMessage
public void whenGettingAMessage(String message)
```

We have opted to receive only text messages (any binary messages coming to this endpoint will be ignored) and to do so in the form of a `String` object. This form is entirely appropriate, as opposed to electing to receive text messages in partial form or in the form of a `java.io.Reader`, as we discussed earlier, because we know that these are only short messages. In fact, in all probability you will elect to receive your text messages in this simplest form on many occasions. You'll see in the implementation of this message handling method that we are first checking whether the message has a particular sequence of bad characters in it. (These traffic signals are, after all, in a family neighborhood!) If all is not OK, it raises a runtime exception with an explanation. If all is OK, the method then checks the message to see if the client is requesting that this server-side endpoint close the connection, in which case it does so after sending the client a message to turn the light red. Finally, if this is any other kind of message, the implementation of this method sends a message to the client indicating that the light should remain green.

If there are bad characters in the message, it sets up an error event that may need to be handled. So the Lifecycle endpoint declares the following method, which will handle any error events:

**Listing:** *Lifecycle Error Event Handling Method Signature*

```
@OnError
public void whenSomethingGoesWrong(Throwable t)
```

This method simply sends the client a message containing a description of the error and asking it to turn the traffic signals yellow. When you run the application, if you send a bad message the Lifecycle message handling method is called. This raises an exception, which in turn causes the error handling method to be called, which in turn lights up the yellow light on the traffic signal. Yellow indicates that traffic can still flow, which is appropriate in this case since the error event did not cause the session to close. There are, of course, many other things you can do in such error handling methods, such as closing the connection by calling the `session.close()` method.

Finally, the Lifecycle endpoint declares the following method, which is to be called whenever the client connection closes:

**Listing:** *Lifecycle Close Event Handling Method Signature*

```
@OnClose
public void whenClosing()
```

You will notice that whether it is the Lifecycle client or the Lifecycle server endpoint that terminates the connection, the `LifecycleEndpoint`'s `whenClosing()` method is called.

# Programmatic Endpoint Lifecycle

Before continuing with the discussion of more aspects of the example we just looked at, let's take a short diversion by looking at the programmatic endpoint version of the WebSocket endpoint lifecycle.

## Lifecycle Events

You will remember from Chapter 1 that programmatic endpoints all must subclass the `javax.websocket.Endpoint` class. You can intercept the open, close, and error events on a programmatic endpoint by providing your own implementation of an `Endpoint` method. Now that you have learned about the WebSocket lifecycle annotations, the following methods of the `Endpoint` class should look pretty familiar to you:

| Event | Endpoint Method |
|-------|-----------------|
| `Open` | `public abstract void onOpen(Session ses,`<br>`                           EndpointConfig config)` |
| `Error` | `public void onError(Session ses, Throwable thr)` |
| `Close` | `public void onClose(Session ses, CloseReason cr)` |

In fact, the only event a programmatic endpoint always has to handle is the open event, which gives it access to the session and the configuration information. The programmatic endpoint is not required to intercept any of the other lifecycle events.

## Handling Messages

By now you are probably wondering how to intercept message events, though of course you have already seen this. In the Java WebSocket API, this works slightly differently because of the wide range of options available to the developer in terms of how you want to handle the messages.

As you saw in the Chapter 1, in order to handle incoming messages, you have to provide a `MessageHandler` implementation. Just as for annotated endpoints, there is a wide range of options for creating different `MessageHandler` implementations to handle different kinds of WebSocket messages in different ways. We will return to examine this full set of options in Chapter 3, but for now we will just note that for handling basic text and binary messages, you only need to implement these:

`MessageHandler.Whole<String>` for text messages, and
`MessageHandler.Whole<ByteBuffer>` for binary messages.

Once you have implemented one or both of these interfaces to define the way you want to consume the messages, all you need to do is register your message handler or message handlers on the `Session` object representing the connection you are interested in listening to by calling

```
session.addMessageHandler(myMessageHandler)
```

sometime before you expect the first message you are interested in to arrive. Typically, endpoints will add their message handlers in the `onOpen()` method so they are sure not to miss any messages.

## Programmatic Lifecycle

Here is the code for the programmatic version of the Lifecycle endpoint:

**Listing:**  *Programmatic Lifecycle WebSocket Endpoint*

```java
import java.io.IOException;
import javax.websocket.CloseReason;
import javax.websocket.Endpoint;
import javax.websocket.EndpointConfig;
import javax.websocket.MessageHandler;
import javax.websocket.Session;

public class ProgrammaticLifecycleEndpoint extends Endpoint {
    private static String START_TIME = "Start Time";
    private Session session;

    @Override
    public  void onOpen(Session session, EndpointConfig config) {
        this.session = session;
        final Session mySession = session;
        this.session.addMessageHandler(new MessageHandler.Whole<String>() {
            @Override
            public void onMessage(String message) {
                if (message.indexOf("xxx") != -1) {
                    throw new IllegalArgumentException("xxx not allowed !");
                } else if (message.indexOf("close") != -1) {
                    try {
                        sendMessage("1:Server closing after " +
                                getConnectionSeconds() + " s");
                        mySession.close();
                    } catch (IOException ioe) {
                        System.out.println("Error closing session "
                                                + ioe.getMessage());
                    }
                    return;
                }
                sendMessage("3:Just processed a message");
            }
        });
        session.getUserProperties().put(START_TIME,
        System.currentTimeMillis());
        this.sendMessage("3:Just opened");
    }

    @Override
    public void onClose(Session session, CloseReason closeReason) {
        System.out.println("Goodbye !");
    }

    @Override
    public void onError(Session session, Throwable thr) {
        this.sendMessage("2:Error: " + thr.getMessage());
    }

}
```

```
void sendMessage(String message) {
    try {
        session.getBasicRemote().sendText(message);
    } catch (IOException ioe) {
        System.out.println("Error sending message " + message);
    }
}

int getConnectionSeconds() {
    long millis = System.currentTimeMillis() -
     ((Long) this.session.getUserProperties().get(START_TIME));
    return (int) millis / 1000;
}
}
```

# Number of Instances and Threading

One thing you may be wondering in this example is why the endpoint uses an instance variable to hold a reference to the `Session` object. You will remember that the `Session` object represents the connection to a single client. You will also notice in the Lifecycle example that we use the session at two points in the lifecycle of the endpoint: once when the new connection from the client is established to mark and remember the time the event occurred, and once in the `whenGettingAMessage()` method when the server endpoint is about to close the connection with the client in order to work out how long the connection was open.

We could easily have written the close handling method like this so that we would not have had to store the session as an instance variable in the open handling method to access it later:

**Listing:** *Alternative Lifecycle Close Event Handling Method Signature*

```
@OnClose
public void whenGettingAMessage(String message, Session session)
```

We could simply have asked for the WebSocket implementation to pass it in.

The reason the Lifecycle example stores the session as an instance variable is that we can use it to illustrate a larger issue about the lifecycle of WebSocket endpoints. If you start up the Lifecycle application again, but this time open up a second browser window to the home page of the same, you will see two sets of traffic signals. If you start pushing the lifecycle buttons in either of the browser windows, you will see that each set of traffic signals can be in a different state. This is because each browser window is acting as a separate client to the Lifecycle WebSocket endpoint, and

because the WebSocket implementation is using a separate instance of the
`LifecycleEndpoint` for each connected client.

What this means is that for each WebSocket endpoint definition, whether
it is an annotated Java class or a programmatic endpoint, the WebSocket
container instantiates a new instance of the endpoint each time a new client
connects. The consequence of this is that each WebSocket endpoint instance
only ever "sees" the same session instance: it is the instance representing
the unique connection from the unique client connected to that endpoint
instance.

You could equally write the Lifecycle sample to take the session into the
`whenGettingAMessage()` method. If you did so, what you would find is
that the instance passed in would be the same `Session` object as the one
that was passed into the `whenOpening(Session session)` method.

There is another important guarantee that the WebSocket implementation
makes for you: no two event threads from the same session (or underlying
connection) are allowed to call an endpoint instance at the same time. This
may sound rather abstract, but what it means is that your endpoint instance
will never be being called by more than one thread from the WebSocket
implementation at a time. It means that if a client sends multiple messages,
the WebSocket implementation must call your endpoint one message at a
time. This is particularly important to know because it means you never have
to worry about programming for concurrent access to your endpoint instance.
It is a key difference between the programming model for Java WebSockets
and the programming model for Java Servlets, in which a Java Servlet instance
may be called simultaneously by multiple threads, each handling a request/
response interaction from a different client. It means that programming
WebSockets is significantly easier!

# Summary

In this chapter, you learned about the events that govern the lifecycle of
WebSocket endpoints. You learned about the sequencing and semantics
of the open, message, error, and close events, as well as the methods and
annotations that allow developers to process these events. Finally, you
learned the threading policy that WebSocket implementations use when they
call developer-created WebSocket endpoints, which means that WebSocket
developers do not usually have to deal with multiple threads calling an
endpoint at the same time.

# CHAPTER
## 3

# Basic Messaging

I n this chapter, we will examine the fundamental aspects of messaging in the Java WebSocket API, which includes many means by which to send and consume messages. We will look at the most straightforward and widespread way to send messages: synchronous sending and receiving of messages. In order to illustrate the concepts and functions we will cover, we will look in detail at the DrawingBoard application. This application uses a Java client front end, so we will introduce the client API of the Java WebSocket API at the same time.

# Messaging Overview

You will remember from Chapter 2 that the WebSocket protocol defines three native message types: text, binary, and ping and pong messages. Let's review all the parts of the Java WebSocket API necessary for sending and receiving messages.

## Sending Messages

In order to send a WebSocket message, the API is the same, whether you are creating an annotated WebSocket endpoint or a programmatic WebSocket endpoint: the `RemoteEndpoint` interface and its subtypes, `RemoteEndpoint.Basic` and `RemoteEndpoint.Async`, hold all the methods for sending messages.

Ping and pong messages are used by developers who wish to check the health of the underlying WebSocket connection. There might be a number of reasons for doing this: they may be checking whether the connection is still active, or they may be making some rough measurement of efficiency by timing how long it takes for the other end of the WebSocket connection to respond with a pong message to a ping message. For now, it's safe to say that many applications will not rely on these kinds of messages. If you do need to send either of these kind of messages, however, the `RemoteEndpoint` instance you obtain from the `Session` object holds the following two methods:

**Listing:** *RemoteEndpoint Sending Pings and Pongs*

```
public void sendPing(ByteBuffer applicationData)
    throws IOException, IllegalArgumentException

public void sendPong(ByteBuffer applicationData)
    throws IOException, IllegalArgumentException
```

The WebSocket specification defines that ping and pong messages may carry 125 bytes of binary data: this is the reason for the `ByteBuffer` parameter on each of the methods. If this limit is exceeded when calling this method with a `ByteBuffer` with more than 125 bytes of binary data in it, an `IllegalArgumentException` will be thrown. As with all the sending methods on the `RemoteEndpoint` interface and its descendants, the `IOException` is used to indicate an error during transmission of the message. This could happen, for example, if the underlying connection turns out to have disconnected prior to making the call to send the message.

Now let's turn to the more common types of messages: text and binary. In Chapter 5, we will examine the APIs and semantics in the Java WebSocket API for sending messages asynchronously; for now, we will limit our review to sending messages synchronously. This means we will need to look at the `RemoteEndpoint.Basic` interface and save our examination of the `RemoteEndpoint.Async` interface until then.

## Sending String Messages

There are three ways to send a `String` using the `RemoteEndpoint.Basic` API. The first, and simplest, is the

**Listing:** *`RemoteEndpoint.Basic` Sending a Text Message*

```
public void sendText(String text) throws IOException
```

method. This method sends the text parameter as a WebSocket text message. This means the other end of the WebSocket connection will receive the message in textual form. The method only returns when the message is sent or throws an error if there was some problem sending it. An example of this might be a broken connection occurring in the middle of the send. We already saw this method in action, both in Chapters 1 and 2; it forms the most basic and frequently used way of sending a WebSocket message.

Since WebSocket messages often take the form of some higher-level object that gets serialized into a `String` in order to be sent, the Java WebSocket API also offers a way to send a `String` message using the familiar Writer API:

**Listing:** *`RemoteEndpoint.Basic` Sending a Text Message to a Stream*

```
public Writer getSendStream() throws IOException
```

This is particularly useful when using other APIs that provide methods to write character data to a writer, for example, the `javax.swing.text.html` `.HTMLEditorKit` API that allows you to write an HTML document to a writer.

Now, the WebSocket protocol allows very large WebSocket messages to be split into smaller pieces. This enables WebSocket implementations to start transmitting messages, even before the whole message has been passed to the implementation by the application, and yield a performance advantage, particularly for applications that send very large messages. In order for developers to be able to take advantage of this kind of partial message transmission, the Java WebSocket API also has the

**Listing:** *RemoteEndpoint Sending a Text Message in Pieces*

```
public void sendText(String partialMessage, boolean isLast)
                                        throws IOException
```

method, which allows developers to send large string messages in a sequence of smaller pieces, each invocation with the `isLast` parameter set to false until the last piece is ready to be sent with the `isLast` parameter set to `true` to indicate that there are no more pieces of this message to send.

## Sending Binary Messages

For the more garden variety application, sending messages in text form can be enough. However, for applications that have a particular data format— like small image files—or applications that require absolutely minimal message sizes, sending messages in binary form is an excellent choice. Fortunately, the Java WebSocket API holds a variety of means of sending messages in binary form. As we did for text messages, we will look only at sending messages synchronously using the `RemoteEndpoint.Basic` interface, deferring our examination of sending messages asynchronously with the `RemoteEndpoint.Async` interface until Chapter 5.

There are three ways to send binary messages. First, we have the two `sendBinary` methods:

**Listing:** *RemoteEndpoint Sending Binary Messages*

```
public void sendBinary(ByteBuffer data) throws IOException

public void sendBinary(ByteBuffer partialByte, boolean isLast)
                                        throws IOException
```

where the `ByteBuffer` method parameter carries the message data. The `IOException` is thrown if there is some communication error that prevents the sending of the message data. As with text messages, the first variant sends the complete message all in one go. The second variant sends a binary message in the form of a sequence of one or more partial binary messages. The `isLast` parameter on this variant is used to indicate whether the partial message being sent is the last one in the sequence that will make up the whole message, or whether there is more to come. This second variant is a good choice if either the message is very large or if creating the message is a process that can be ongoing while you send the first parts of the message that are ready to go.

**NOTE**
*For both binary and text messages, this form of sending a message as a sequence of partial messages can have some powerful performance gains for some applications. However, the exact form in which the message is ultimately transmitted is up to the WebSocket implementation. Some implementations may transmit a large message in a large number of small pieces, and some implementations may transmit a large message as a small number of larger pieces. Some implementations may let you configure this aspect of their implementation. Others may even tune these parameters based on local network conditions! So it is always worth doing a little experimentation and testing before arriving at the variant that works most efficiently for your application and the WebSocket implementation it is running on.*

Finally, you may obtain a reference to a `java.io.OutputStream` to which you can write binary message data. This can be useful, especially when working with Java APIs that write data objects directly to Java I/O APIs. It is your responsibility to close the output stream once you are done writing your message to it. Once you close the output stream, the message is sent. In order to use this mode of sending binary messages, you will be using this method:

**Listing:** `RemoteEndpoint.Basic` *Sending a Binary Message Using a Stream*

```
public OutputStream getSendStream() throws IOException
```

## Sending Java Objects as Messages

Now that you have seen that there are several ways to send messages in either text or binary form, it's worth noting that there is a large class of applications for which this is sufficient. Such applications tend to send rather simple messages: perhaps simple stock updates, a temperature measurement, or news headlines, for example; but there are also many WebSocket applications that send a more complex form of messages. Those messages might include both data and an instruction or qualification. They might contain data that is highly structured. For this kind of application, it is extremely useful to be able to model those messages, not as text or binary data, but as higher-level Java objects.

The Java WebSocket API allows you to send any kind of Java object using the `RemoteEndpoint.Basic` method call:

**Listing:** `RemoteEndpoint.Basic` *Sending a Java Object*

```
public void sendObject(Object data) throws IOException, EncodeException
```

You may be wondering how the WebSocket implementation turns this object into a WebSocket message. (As you read in Chapter 2, only three basic flavors of WebSocket message can be sent on the wire: text, binary, or one of the heartbeat messages, ping or pong.) The answer is that it depends on what kind of object you pass in.

If you pass in a Java primitive (or boxed equivalent), the WebSocket implementation will turn the data into a standard Java representation as a `String` (that is, a `toString()` representation).

If you pass in any other object, you will need to provide the WebSocket implementation an implementation of one of the `javax.websocket.Encoder` interfaces. You'll see an example of this later in the chapter, but for now, let's take a quick look at one of them. The most common interface in the encoder family is the `javax.websocket.Encoder.Text<T>` interface, where *T* is the class of the object you want to send. The main method of the interface is shown here:

**Listing:** *The encode Method of the* `Encoder.Text<T>` *Interface*

```
public String encode(T object) throws EncodeException
```

Each time you try to send an object of type *T* using the `sendObject` method of `RemoteEndpoint.Basic`, the WebSocket implementation will call the encoder you provide here with the object. The string you return out of your implementation of the `encode()` method is the one that actually will be sent to the remote endpoint. If your encoder is unable to encode as a string the object provided, you may throw an `EncodeException`. Returning to the `sendObject()` method of `RemoteEndpoint.Basic`, this is the `EncodeException` that would be thrown from this method in this situation.

There are other `Encoder` interfaces you can choose as alternatives. For example, if you want to encode your objects as binary WebSocket messages, you can implement the `Encoder.Binary<T>` interface. If you want to encode your object to Java I/O streams, you can implement either `Encoder.CharacterStream<T>` or `Encoder.BinaryStream<T>`.

Once you have created the encoder you want to use, you have a choice as to how to configure it on your endpoint.

For annotated endpoints, all you need to do is declare the `Encoder` class on the class-level WebSocket annotation you use. Let's say you have an Orchard application that needs to send a message which is an instance of a class in the application called "Apple." For example, to configure an encoder on a server endpoint that knows how to encode `Apple` objects in the application, you might use the following annotation:

**Listing:** *Specifying an encoder in the* `@ServerEndpoint` *Annotation*

```
@ServerEndpoint(
    value = "/fruit_trees",
    encoders = { MyAppleEncoder.class }
)
```

Once you do this, whenever you obtain a reference to a `RemoteEndpoint` from this annotated endpoint, you may pass an `Apple` object into its `sendObject()` method, and the WebSocket implementation will use your `MyAppleEncoder` implementation to encode the `Apple` object into a WebSocket message.

If you are using programmatic endpoints, you can configure your encoder classes when you create the `EndpointConfig` object you need to provide in order to deploy the endpoint. For example, if you are creating a programmatic client endpoint that needs to use the `MyAppleEncoder` encoder implementation that we used as an example above, you would need to include the following code:

**Listing:** *Configuring an Encoder for a Programmatic Client Endpoint*

```
List<Class<? extends Encoder>> encoders = new ArrayList<>();
encoders.add(MyAppleEncoder.class);
ClientEndpointConfig config =
    ClientEndpointConfig.Builder.create()
                              .encoders(encoders)
                              .build();
```

As you will see in the DrawingBoard application we will look at later in this chapter, you will need to create a `ClientEndpointConfig` instance in order to deploy the client endpoint it will use.

Now, whenever you obtain a reference to a `RemoteEndpoint` from this programmatic endpoint, you will be able to call its `sendObject()` method with an `Apple` instance. The WebSocket implementation will use the `MyAppleEncoder` implementation you provided to encode the `Apple` instance into a WebSocket message.

We will conclude our examination of how to send custom Java objects as WebSocket messages using the `RemoteEndpoint` interface with a table that summarizes all the possible types of `Encoder` interfaces you can choose to implement and configure for your endpoint.

| Encoder Interface | Conversion | Primary Method |
|---|---|---|
| Encoder.Text<T> | *T* to `String` | `String encode(T object)` `throws EncodeException` |
| Encoder .TextStream<T> | *T* to `Writer` | `void encode(T object,` `Writer writer)` `throws EncodeException,` `IOException` |
| Encoder .Binary<T> | *T* to `ByteBuffer` | `ByteBuffer encode(T object)` `throws EncodeException` |
| Encoder .BinaryStream | *T* to `OutputStream` | `void encode(T object,` `OutputStream os)` `throws EncodeException,` `IOException` |

# Receiving WebSocket Messages

Now that we have taken a look at some of the ways in which a WebSocket application can send messages, let's turn the tables and look at the ways in which a WebSocket endpoint can elect to receive messages.

## Receiving WebSocket Messages in Annotated Endpoints

We saw in Chapter 1 that the simplest way to receive a text message for annotated endpoints is to write a Java method that takes a `String` parameter and mark the method with the `@OnMessage` annotation, as shown here:

**Listing:**   *Handling a Text Message with @OnMessage*

```
@OnMessage
public void handleTextMessages(String textMessage) {
        return "I got this " + textMessage + " !");
}
```

This is the simplest but not the only form in which you can choose to receive text messages in this endpoint. You can elect to receive binary WebSocket messages and pong messages by simply using an appropriate method parameter to "catch" them. In order to receive a binary message, the easiest way to do so is to use a `byte[]` array parameter:

**Listing:**   *Handling a Binary Message with @OnMessage*

```
@OnMessage
public String handleBinaryMessages(byte[] messageData) {
        return "I got " + messageData.length + " bytes of data !";
}
```

In order to receive pong messages, you simply declare a method parameter of type `javax.websocket.PongMessage`. For example:

**Listing:**   *Handling a Pong Message with @OnMessage*

```
@OnMessage
public String handlePongMessages(PongMessage pongMessage) {
        return "I got a pong message carrying " +
                    pongMessage.getApplicationData().length +
                                " bytes of data !");
}
```

These three variants cover the main two WebSocket message types, text and binary, and how to catch incoming pong messages.

**NOTE**
*What happened to listening to ping messages?*
*You may be wondering at this point why we have not looked at a way to listen to incoming ping messages: the answer is that the Java WebSocket API does not have a way to do so! WebSocket implementations are required to answer any incoming ping messages on a connection (for example, one you sent manually using the* sendPing() *method on a* RemoteEndpoint) *for you with a pong message containing the same data as soon as they possibly can. So there is never a need for you to explicitly write code to listen for ping messages.*

Very similar to the variants for sending messages and for processing text and binary messages, there are a number of variants on how you can elect to receive them. Just as for sending messages, you are able to receive messages in the form of a sequence of partial messages. For example, if you know that the other end of your WebSocket session is going to send you very large messages, it is likely that each message will be broken up into a sequence of smaller ones by the WebSocket implementation. In this case, you can elect to receive each partial message as it arrives, rather than having to wait for the whole thing. In this case, you would declare a method like this:

**Listing:**  *Handling a Text Message Arriving in Pieces with* @OnMessage

```
@OnMessage
public void handlePartial(String textMessagePart, boolean isLast)
```

where each time a new part of the message arrives, the WebSocket implementation calls this method with the message part in the textMessagePart parameter, and the boolean isLast flag set to false if there is more to come, or to true if this part is the last part arriving. You can use a similar form for binary messages as well, as you are about to see.

The following table gives a listing of how annotated endpoint methods can receive incoming text, binary, and pong WebSocket messages in the most familiar forms for Java developers:

| Parameter Type | Message Type Handled | Example |
|---|---|---|
| `String` | Text message | `public void handle(String`<br>`                 message)` |
| `String, boolean` | Partial text message | `public void handle(`<br>`    String partialMessage,`<br>`           boolean isLast)` |
| `Reader` | Text message as stream | `public void handle(`<br>`           Reader message)` |
| `byte[]` | Binary message | `public void handle(byte[] data)` |
| `ByteBuffer` | Binary message | `public void handle(`<br>`           ByteBuffer data)` |
| `byte[], boolean` | Partial binary message | `public void handle(`<br>`        byte[] partialData,`<br>`        boolean isLast)` |
| `ByteBuffer, boolean` | Partial binary message | `public void handle(`<br>`    ByteBuffer partialData,`<br>`              boolean isLast)` |
| `PongMessage` | Pong message | `public void handle(`<br>`    PongMessage pong)` |

We mentioned earlier that many WebSocket applications will want to deal with data objects that are richer in structure than `String` or unstructured data. Fortunately, for those applications the Java WebSocket API also provides support to allow developers to receive messages in the form of arbitrary Java objects, provided the developer also provides a decoder class so that the WebSocket implementation knows how to transform the WebSocket message coming off the wire into the Java object the developer asked for. For example, if you want to receive a message in the form of a Java object of class `Orange` that you have created, you would write a method like the following on your annotated endpoint:

**Listing:** *Handling a Java Object Message with @OnMessage*

```
@OnMessage
public void addToBasket(Orange orange) {
      this.bag.addShoppingItem(orange);
      this.cost = this.cost + orange.getPrice();
}
```

For this to work, the WebSocket implementation must know how to convert an incoming message into an `Orange` object, and to do this you must provide an implementation of the `Decoder` interface. As with `Encoder` interfaces, there's a variety of possible subtypes you can implement. For now, we will illustrate the general concept by looking at the `Decoder.Text<T>` interface, which governs how the WebSocket implementation will decode an incoming text message into a Java object of type *T*. In our example, the primary method of the `Decoder.Text<Orange>` interface you need to implement is `decode()`:

**Listing:** *The decode() Method Signature of the Decoder.Text<Orange> Interface*

```
public Orange decode(String rawMessage) throws DecodeException
```

The interface will also require you to implement the `willDecode()` method:

**Listing:** *The willDecode() Method Signature of the Decoder.Text<Orange> Interface*

```
public boolean willDecode(String s)
```

This method is always called by the WebSocket implementation prior to the calling to `decode()` in order for you to have the chance to skip decoding any text message that is obviously in the wrong format.

There are a number of subtypes of the `Decoder` interface that allow you to differentiate between which kinds of WebSocket messages you wish to convert into Java objects, and to some extent between the modes by which you convert them. The following table gives a summary of all the `Decoder` interfaces and what they are used for, where you want to receive messages in the form of *T* objects:

| Decoder Interface | Conversion | Primary Decode Method |
|---|---|---|
| `Decoder.Text<T>` | `String` to *T* | `T decode(String raw)` `throws DecodeException` |
| `Decoder.TextStream<T>` | `Reader` to *T* | `T decode(Reader raw)` `throws DecodeException` |
| `Decoder.Binary` | `ByteBuffer` to *T* | `T decode(ByteBuffer raw)` `throws DecodeException` |
| `Decoder.BinaryStream` | `InputStream` to *T* | `T decode(InputStream raw)` `throws DecodeException` |

You'll notice that you may throw a `DecodeException` if the raw data you are asked to decode cannot be turned into the Java object you wish. In all such decoding failures, the incoming message that caused the failure will not be delivered, but the `DecodeException` that is generated in the decoder will be delivered to the error handling method of the endpoint.

**TIP**
*Always include an error handling method in your WebSocket endpoints. Runtime exceptions generated in other WebSocket methods on your endpoint, such as the open event handling method, will be passed here, in addition to any errors processing incoming messages. If you don't have an error handling method, you may not know that a message has not arrived!*

One convenience provided by the Java WebSocket API is built-in text decoders for the Java primitive types and their class equivalents. The approach the WebSocket implementations take is to use the standard Java string representation of the primitive type or class equivalent. This means that the decode operation is equivalent to the Java primitive class equivalent that would be constructed using the single `String` parameter constructor of the class. For example, if a developer wrote a method hoping to handle incoming text messages in the form of Java integers, like this:

**Listing:**   *Handling an Integer-Valued WebSocket Message with `@OnMessage`*

```
@OnMessage
public void doCount(Integer message) {
        // process Integer
}
```

an incoming text message string arriving on the wire with value `42` would result in a call to the `doCount()` method above with `Integer` equal to `new Integer(42)`.

The following table summarizes the delivery options for messages as Java objects other than the standard text, binary, and `PongMessage` forms listed earlier, either as a Java primitive or class equivalent, or as a custom Java object defined by the developer.

| Delivery Option | Decoder | Example |
| --- | --- | --- |
| Text message as Java primitive or class equivalent | Automatic | `@OnMessage`<br>`public void handleTransferCode(`<br>`                        Double d)` |
| Text or binary message as custom Java object | Developer provided | `@OnMessage`<br>`public void handleObject(`<br>`                    CustomObject o)` |

Before we leave the topic of receiving messages in annotated endpoints, we should cover one last topic that is very closely related to the method forms that may be annotated with `@OnMessage`.

In all the examples so far, the return types of the `@OnMessage` methods have been `void`. However, you will remember from the Chapter 1 Echo sample that there is a very convenient way to respond immediately to an incoming WebSocket message, and that is to provide a return value on the method you annotate with `@OnMessage`. The return type dictates the kind of WebSocket message that the WebSocket implementation will send back to the sender of the incoming message.

In order to respond with a text message, the return type should be `String`. In order to respond with a binary message, the return type should be `byte[]` or `ByteBuffer`. Finally, you are allowed to respond with text messages that are the standard Java representation of Java primitives or their class equivalents by using the same conversion rules we have already discussed in this chapter. This means that all the following methods are valid message handling methods on an annotated endpoint:

**Listing:** *Example Message Handling Methods*

```
@OnMessage
public String echo(String message) { ... }
@OnMessage
public Integer processAndConfirm(byte[] upload) { ... }
@OnMessage
public boolean purchase(String item) { ... }
```

**Multiple Message Handling Methods**   We have seen that there is a wide variety of ways in which you can consume incoming messages on an annotated WebSocket endpoint. You wonder at some point what happens if you use more than one of those ways on the same annotated endpoint.

In order for the Java WebSocket implementation to be able to map an incoming message to the correct message handling method on an annotated endpoint, it places a hard restriction on how these modes may be combined, which is that each annotated endpoint may have at most one message handling method per native WebSocket message type: text, binary, and pong.

The upshot of this is that, for example, you cannot have two methods annotated with @OnMessage indicating that both wish to handle text messages. For example, you may not have an annotated endpoint that declares the following:

**Listing:** *Illegal Use of Multiple Message Handling Methods*

```
@ServerEndpoint(
        value="/orchard",
        decoders= {OrangeDecoder.class}
)
public class FruitTree {
        @OnMessage
        public void handleString(String message) {
                ...
        }
        @OnMessage
        public void handleOrange(Orange orange) {
                ...
        }
}
```

where OrangeDecoder implements either Decoder.Text<Orange> or Decoder.TextStream<Orange>. This example violates the rule of having at most one message handling method per native WebSocket message type, because it has two methods for handling incoming text messages. If you tried to deploy such an endpoint, you would find that doing so would cause a deployment error and your endpoint would not be deployed. To make the above example a valid annotated endpoint, you would need to start by separating the two message handling methods onto two distinct annotated endpoints.

## Receiving WebSocket Messages in Programmatic Endpoints

Now that we have taken a comprehensive look at how to handle incoming WebSocket messages on annotated endpoints in a variety of forms, let's turn to how to handle incoming messages on the sibling of the annotated endpoint, the programmatic endpoint.

All the means by which a programmatic endpoint can receive messages hinge on the `MessageHandler` interface and its subtypes. For example, in order to receive text messages in the form of a Java `String` object, you will recall from Chapter 1's programmatic Echo example that we need to implement the `MessageHandler.Whole<String>` interface and add the message handler to the current `Session` object in the programmatic endpoint's onOpen method:

**Listing:** *Handling a Text Message in a Programmatic Endpoint*

```
public void onOpen(Session session, EndpointConfig endpointConfig) {
        final Session mySession = session;
        mySession.addMessageHandler(new MessageHandler.Whole<String>() {
            @Override
            public void onMessage(String text) {
              handleTextMessage(text);
              }
        });
    }

private void handleTextMessage(String text) {
        // handle incoming messages here
}
```

As you may have come to expect with the Java WebSocket API, there are a number of ways you can elect to process incoming messages in programmatic WebSocket endpoints. Whichever way you choose, you will always require the following two steps:

1. Implement some subtype of *MessageHandler*, depending on the type of message you want to handle and how you want to handle it. You may elect to receive whole WebSocket messages or receive WebSocket messages as sequences of partial messages.

2. Configure your *MessageHandler* implementation on the current *Session* object in your programmatic endpoint. Usually, you will do this once when the new session is created within the onOpen() method, although it is possible to swap out *MessageHandler* implementations at other points in the endpoint's lifecycle.

The following table lists all the variants of `MessageHandler` and describes the types of incoming messages they will consume and how they will present them to the programmatic endpoint that uses them.

| MessageHandler | Message Type | Delivery As |
|---|---|---|
| `MessageHandler` `.Whole<String>` | Text | Java `String` object |
| `MessageHandler` `.Whole<Reader>` | Text | Java I/O stream |
| `MessageHandler` `.Whole<ByteBuffer>` | Binary | Java NIO `ByteBuffer` |
| `MessageHandler` `.Whole<byte[]>` | Binary | Byte array |
| `MessageHandler` `.Whole<InputStream>` | Binary | Java I/O stream |
| `MessageHandler` `.Partial<String>` | Partial text | Sequence of Java strings |
| `MessageHandler` `.Partial<ByteBuffer>` | Partial binary | Sequence of `ByteBuffers` |
| `MessageHandler` `.Partial<byte[]>` | Partial binary | Sequence of byte arrays |

If something looks familiar here, it is because the options for consuming incoming WebSocket messages in programmatic endpoints are the same as for annotated endpoints.

Just as for annotated endpoints, you may elect to receive incoming WebSocket messages in the form of a Java object of your choosing. If you do so, you must provide an implementation of the `Decoder` interface able to perform the conversion from native WebSocket message to your Java object. So, to the preceding table we add the following option:

| MessageHandler | Message Type | Delivery As |
|---|---|---|
| `MessageHandler.Whole<T>` with `Decoder.Text<T>` or `Decoder.TextStream<T>` | Text | Object type *T* |
| `MessageHandler.Whole<T>` with `Decoder.Binary<T>` or `Decoder.BinaryStream<T>` | Binary | Object type *T* |

Similar to configuring `Encoder` implementations on a programmatic endpoint, any `Decoder` implementations you provide in order to support a `MessageHandler`-receiving custom object have to be configured at deployment time. For example, in order to configure the `OrangeDecoder` we used earlier in the annotation example to a programmatic endpoint deployed in a WAR file, we can use the following example of a `ServerApplicationConfig` implementation, which does just that:

**Listing:** *Configuring `Decoders` in a Programmatic Server Endpoint*

```
public class MyServerApplicationConfig implements ServerApplicationConfig {

    public Set<ServerEndpointConfig> getEndpointConfigs(
                      Set<Class<? extends Endpoint>> endpointClasses) {
        Set<ServerEndpointConfig> configs = new HashSet<>();
        List<Class<? extends Decoder>> decoders = new ArrayList<>();
        decoders.add(MyOrangeDecoder.class);
        ServerEndpointConfig config =
            ServerEndpointConfig.Builder.create(MyEndpoint.class, "/fruit")
                                .decoders(decoders)
                                .build();
        configs.add(config);
        return configs;

    }

    public Set<Class<?>> getAnnotatedEndpointClasses(Set<Class<?>> sc) {
        return sc;
    }

}
```

We end with a final note of caution to conclude this survey of how you can elect to receive WebSocket messages in a programmatic endpoint. The Java WebSocket API allows you to register only one `MessageHandler` per native WebSocket message type per `Session` for a programmatic endpoint. This is so that WebSocket implementations can easily determine which `MessageHandler` to call when a WebSocket message arrives. The consequence of this for developers is that when making the call to

```
session.addMessageHandler(myMessageHandler)
```

a `java.lang.IllegalStateException` will be thrown if there is a `MessageHandler` already registered for the WebSocket message type (text, binary, or pong) that the `myMessageHandler` `MessageHandler` consumes.

You have probably noticed that this restriction mirrors the situation we covered earlier with annotated endpoints wherein each annotated endpoint is allowed at most only one method to handle each native WebSocket message type.

**NOTE**
*In order to determine the native type of the WebSocket messages consumed by a particular* `MessageHandler`, *you may need to look at the accompanying* `Decoder` *to see whether it is decoding text or binary messages. Or both!*

# DrawingBoard Application

In this section, we will bring together many of the concepts and details we have surveyed in the form of a sample application.

The DrawingBoard sample is a multi-client/server Java WebSocket application. The client-side of the application is a Java Swing application that contains a client Java WebSocket endpoint. It presents a simple drawing canvas on which the user can draw a variety of different shapes of different sizes and colors. The server side of the DrawingBoard application is a web application containing a single server-side Java WebSocket endpoint. Whenever the user draws a shape on the drawing board, the client sends the server an update. When the server receives the update, it broadcasts to all other connected clients the nature of the update it just received. As the clients get updates from the server, they update their drawing canvases to reflect the changes made in the original drawing client. In this way, all connected clients are actually collaborating on a group drawing. Figure 3-1 shows two client windows collaborating on drawing a pastoral scene.

## DrawingBoard Client

Let's take a look first at the client WebSocket endpoint. All of our annotated endpoints up to this point have been server-side endpoints, so this DrawingBoard client endpoint is our first look at a client WebSocket endpoint. Instead of the `@ServerEndpoint`, for the client endpoint we use the `@ClientEndpoint`. This class-level annotation is the client-side equivalent of the `@ServerEndpoint` annotation. Once you have annotated

**FIGURE 3-1.** *Two DrawingBoard users collaborating*

a Java class with this annotation, just as for a server-side annotated endpoint, you can use any or all of the method-level annotations to intercept lifecycle events and WebSocket messages.

Before we look at the client endpoint, let's take a look at the code that represents the drawing objects in the application. They are represented by the DrawingObject and Shape class. Here is the DrawingObject class:

**Listing:** *The DrawingObject Class*

```
import java.awt.*;

public class DrawingObject {
    public static String MESSAGE_NAME = "DrawingObject";
    private Shape shape;
    private Point center;
    private int radius = 0;
    private Color color;

    public DrawingObject(Shape shape, Point center, int radius, Color color) {
        this.shape = shape;
        this.center = center;
        this.radius = radius;
        this.color = color;
    }

    public Shape getShape() {
        return this.shape;
    }

    public Point getCenter() {
        return this.center;
    }

    public int getRadius() {
        return this.radius;
    }

    public Color getColor() {
        return this.color;
    }

    public void draw(Graphics g) {
        g.setColor(this.color);
        switch (shape) {
            case CIRCLE:
                g.fillOval(center.x - radius,
                            center.y - radius, 2 * radius,
                                        2 * radius);
                break;
            case TRIANGLE:
                Polygon triangle = new Polygon();
                triangle.addPoint(center.x, center.y-radius);
```

```
                triangle.addPoint(center.x+radius, center.y+radius);
                triangle.addPoint(center.x-radius, center.y+radius);
                g.fillPolygon(triangle);
                break;
            case SQUARE:
                Polygon square = new Polygon();
                square.addPoint(center.x-radius, center.y-radius);
                square.addPoint(center.x+radius, center.y-radius);
                square.addPoint(center.x+radius, center.y+radius);
                square.addPoint(center.x-radius, center.y+radius);
                g.fillPolygon(square);
                break;
            case PENTAGON:
                Polygon pentagon = new Polygon();
                pentagon.addPoint(center.x, center.y-radius);
                pentagon.addPoint(center.x+radius, center.y-(radius/5));
                pentagon.addPoint(center.x+(3*radius/5), center.y+radius);
                pentagon.addPoint(center.x-(3*radius/5), center.y+radius);
                pentagon.addPoint(center.x-radius, center.y-(radius/5));
                g.fillPolygon(pentagon);
            default:
                g.fillOval(center.x - 5, center.y - 5, 10, 10);
                break;
        }
    }

}
```

and the accompanying Shape enum that it uses:

---

**Listing:** *The Shape Class*

```
public enum Shape {
    CIRCLE,
    TRIANGLE,
    SQUARE,
    PENTAGON;

    @Override
    public String toString() {
        if (this == CIRCLE) {
            return "Circle";
        } else if (this == TRIANGLE) {
            return "Triangle";
        } else if (this == SQUARE) {
            return "Square";
        } else if (this == PENTAGON) {
            return "Pentagon";
        } else {
            return "unknown";
        }
    }
}
```

```
    public static Shape fromString(String s) {
        for (Shape shape : Shape.values()) {
            if (shape.toString().equals(s)) {
                return shape;
            }
        }
        throw new IllegalArgumentException("Cannot make shape from: " + s);
    }

}
```

We can see from the `DrawingObject` class that images drawing on the canvas have a few simple properties: the shape type, the origin on the canvas, a radius dictating how large the shape is, and a color attribute.

Now let's look at the client endpoint that is behind the Java Swing window that forms the DrawingBoard client.

**Listing:**    *The `DrawingClient` Class*

```
import java.io.*;
import java.net.*;
import javax.websocket.*;
import jwsp.chapter3.drawing.data.DrawingDecoder;
import jwsp.chapter3.drawing.data.DrawingEncoder;
import jwsp.chapter3.drawing.data.DrawingObject;

@ClientEndpoint(
    decoders = { DrawingDecoder.class },
    encoders = { DrawingEncoder.class }
)
public class DrawingClient {
    private Session session;
    private DrawingWindow window;

    public DrawingClient(DrawingWindow window) {
        this.window = window;
    }

    @OnOpen
    public void init(Session session) {
        this.session = session;
    }

    @OnMessage
    public void drawingChanged(DrawingObject drawingObject) {
        window.addDrawingObject(drawingObject);
    }

    public void notifyServerDrawingChanged(DrawingObject drawingObject) {
        try {
            this.session.getBasicRemote().sendObject(drawingObject);
        } catch (IOException ioe) {
            System.out.println("Error: IO " + ioe.getMessage());
```

```
        } catch (EncodeException ee) {
            System.out.println("Error encoding object: " + ee.getObject());
        }
    }

    @OnError
    public void handleError(Throwable thw) {
        if (thw instanceof DecodeException) {
            System.out.println("Error decoding incoming message: "
                                + ((DecodeException)thw).getText());
        } else {
            System.out.println("Client WebSocket error: " +
                                            thw.getMessage());
        }
    }

    public static DrawingClient connect(DrawingWindow window, String path) {
        WebSocketContainer wsc = ContainerProvider.getWebSocketContainer();
        try {
            DrawingClient client = new DrawingClient(window);
            wsc.connectToServer(client, new URI(path));
            return client;
        } catch (IOException ioe) {
            System.out.println("Error Connecting: " + ioe.getMessage());
        } catch (DeploymentException de) {
            System.out.println("Error deploying: " + de.getMessage());
        } catch (URISyntaxException ue) {
            System.out.println("Bad path: " + path);
        }
        return null;
    }

    public void disconnect() {
        if (this.session != null) {
            try {
                this.session.close();
            } catch (IOException ioe) {
                System.out.println("Error closing the session: " + ioe);
            }
        }
    }
}
```

First, we note that this client endpoint can only be created by passing in a DrawingWindow object. The DrawingWindow is a Swing JFrame that contains all the user interface controls and the drawing canvas we see onscreen when we run the client side of the DrawingBoard application. The client endpoint stores the reference to the DrawingWindow as a private instance variable for use later after it has been constructed. We can see here that the client endpoint is going to make use of two classes to encode and decode the messages it sends and receives: the DrawingEncoder class and the DrawingDecoder class. These classes know how to encode a DrawingObject into a WebSocket message and how to decode a WebSocket message into a DrawingObject, respectively. We will look at how these conversion classes are implemented shortly, but for now we will just note that in this client endpoint we are configuring them for use on the client endpoint by listing them in the @ClientEndpoint annotation. Other than that, the client endpoint is making use of two of the WebSocket lifecycle events. First, it is intercepting the open even by the use of the @OnOpen annotation on its init(Session session) method. The method is storing the Session object provided to it when the WebSocket connection with the server is established as a private instance variable for use later. The second lifecycle annotation this client endpoint uses is the @OnMessage annotation on its drawingChanged(DrawingObject drawingObject) method. Because this WebSocket endpoint has a Decoder configured for DrawingObjects, we are able to use the DrawingObject as a parameter on this method. So, in this case, WebSocket messages will be converted into DrawingObjects when they are received, and this method will be called. We can see from the implementation of the drawingChanged() method that in response to receiving a DrawingObject message from the server, this client endpoint will ask the DrawingWindow to which it refers to draw the object that was sent. We see also that the client endpoint has declared an error handling method by means of the @OnError annotation.

Next, we see that the DrawingEndpoint holds the method notifyServerDrawingChanged(DrawingObject drawingObject), which sends the server side of the DrawingBoard application an instance of DrawingObject by invoking the sendObject() call on the RemoteEndpoint representing the server side of the application. Under the covers, the WebSocket implementation is using the encoder provided in the class-level @ClientEndpoint annotation, that is, an instance of DrawingEncoder. The encode method of DrawingEncoder will be called at runtime in order to transform the DrawingObject instance passed into a WebSocket message.

Notice that the error handling method, handleError(), of the DrawingClient explicitly handles any errors that arise from errors decoding incoming messages separately from other kinds of connection errors. Of course, in a real application, such error handling will involve a little more than printing the error to output, but the handleError() method shows you how you can separate out this kind of error in your code.

Finally, we note that the DrawingClient class has a static method connect() that connects it to the server. The beef of the method implementation is the connectToServer() method on the

WebSocketContainer class, which deploys the instance of the client endpoint to the URL provided.

Next, we turn to the DrawingWindow itself. This is the user interface that uses the DrawingClient endpoint as its model. We will not spend a lot of time talking through how the user interface is put together, since this a book about Java WebSockets and not the Java Swing APIs. But we will note that the events of interest generated by the DrawingWindow are as follows:

1. The call to the DrawingClient class initiates the connection to the server side of the application using the static connect() method we examined earlier. This is done by the drawing window as it opens.

2. Each time the user draws a new object on the drawing canvas of the DrawingWindow, the DrawingWindow asks the DrawingClient endpoint to notify the server by calling its notifyServerDrawingChanged() method with an instance of the DrawingObject that the DrawingWindow created.

3. As the DrawingWindow closes, it calls the disconnect() method on the DrawingClient we mentioned above, which closes the session with the server.

These are the main points of contact between the DrawingWindow and the DrawingClient endpoint that it uses to stay in sync with the group drawing effort. We do not list the DrawingWindow code here in the interest of keeping to the topic of WebSockets, since it is primarily user interface code.

We'll pause here to take a look at the DrawingEncoder and DrawingDecoder classes that the DrawingClient uses.

First, here is the DrawingEncoder whose job it is to turn a drawing object into a WebSocket message:

**Listing:**   *The DrawingEncoder Class*

```
import javax.websocket.EncodeException;
import javax.websocket.Encoder;
import javax.websocket.EndpointConfig;

public class DrawingEncoder implements Encoder.Text<DrawingObject> {

    @Override
    public void init(EndpointConfig config) {}
```

```
@Override
public void destroy() {}

@Override
public String encode(DrawingObject drawingObject)
                                   throws EncodeException {
    StringBuilder sb = new StringBuilder();
    sb.append(DrawingObject.MESSAGE_NAME);
    sb.append(",");
    sb.append(drawingObject.getShape().toString());
    sb.append(",");
    sb.append(drawingObject.getCenter().x);
    sb.append(",");
    sb.append(drawingObject.getCenter().y);
    sb.append(",");
    sb.append(drawingObject.getRadius());
    sb.append(",");
    sb.append(drawingObject.getColor().getRGB());
    return sb.toString();
}

}
```

Notice that the DrawingEncoder implements the
Encoder.Text<DrawingObject> interface. This tells you right away
that it is encoding a DrawingObject, the parameter to the interface it
implements, and that the kind of WebSocket message to which it encodes
the DrawingObject is a text message.

**TIP**

*To quickly determine what kind of conversion a
Java WebSocket Encoder or Decoder performs,
just take a look at the particular Encoder or
Decoder interface it implements.*

You will see that the Encoder interface defines a little lifecycle of its
own. The init(EndpointConfig config) and destroy() methods are
called as each encoder instance is being brought into service and after the
implementation has finished using it. This can be useful if the encoder you
are implementing needs to initialize and/or cleanup expensive resources it
may have used. The meat of the implementation is in the encode() method,
which turns the drawing object into a string that is a comma-separated listing
of all the properties of the DrawingObject.

As we shall see at the end of this chapter, like endpoints themselves, WebSocket implementations will create one instance of encoders per peer connection. So in our DrawingBoard application, there will be one DrawingEncoder instance for each DrawingWindow, since each DrawingWindow connects to one peer, the DrawingServer endpoint. In this DrawingEncoder, the implementations of the lifecycle methods are empty since no such resources are needed.

Now let's look at the converse operation. When the DrawingObject is encoded, it is turned into a WebSocket text message by the DrawingEncoder and sent to the server. When the server sends out its update of a new DrawingObject, having been added to the group canvas, it sends a WebSocket text message out to all the connected clients, each of which uses a DrawingDecoder to convert the text message containing the DrawingObject data into a DrawingObject instance.

**Listing:** *The DrawingDecoder Class*

```
import java.awt.Color;
import java.awt.Point;
import java.util.StringTokenizer;
import javax.websocket.Decoder;
import javax.websocket.EndpointConfig;
import javax.websocket.DecodeException;

public class DrawingDecoder implements Decoder.Text<DrawingObject> {

    @Override
    public void init(EndpointConfig config) {}

    @Override
    public void destroy() {}

    @Override
    public DrawingObject decode(String s) throws DecodeException {
        StringTokenizer st = new StringTokenizer(s, ",");
        String message_name = st.nextToken();
        Shape shape = Shape.fromString(st.nextToken());
        Point center = new Point(new Integer(st.nextToken()),
                                 new Integer(st.nextToken()));
        int radius = new Integer(st.nextToken());
        Color color = new Color(new Integer(st.nextToken()));
        return new DrawingObject(shape, center, radius, color);
    }
}
```

```
@Override
public boolean willDecode(String s) {
    return s.startsWith(DrawingObject.MESSAGE_NAME);
}

}
```

Again, you can see that the `DrawingDecoder` does not need to take advantage of the lifecycle `init()` and `destroy()` methods of the `Decoder` interface, and you can see immediately that because the `DrawingDecoder` implements the `Decoder.Text<DrawingObject>` interface, the contract it must uphold is to convert WebSocket text messages into `DrawingObject` instances—exactly the opposite process of the `DrawingEncoder`. The implementation of the `willDecode()` method makes a preliminary look of the text message to sanity-check that it is likely to be something it can decode. If the `willDecode()` method does not return `true`, the WebSocket implementation will not attempt to call the `decode()` method and the message will not be able to be delivered as a `DrawingObject`. However, if the `willDecode()` test passes, the WebSocket implementation will go on to call the `decode()` method, passing in the text message. You can see the implementation of `decode()` that we have in `DrawingDecoder` breaks up the text message into the constituent properties of the drawing object, using the comma as a separator, and reconstructs the `DrawingObject` instance it returns from those properties. This is exactly the opposite process of the `DrawingEncoder` that we expected it to be.

At this point, we understand nearly all of the application!

## The DrawingServer Endpoint

Let's move on to looking at the server side. You will see right away by the use of the `@ServerEndpoint` that the `DrawingServer` class is an annotated WebSocket endpoint mapped to the URI /`draw`, relative to the context root of the containing WAR file.

**Listing:**  *The `DrawingServer` Class*

```
import java.awt.Color;
import java.io.IOException;
import java.io.Reader;
import java.util.Iterator;
import javax.websocket.*;
import javax.websocket.server.ServerEndpoint;
import jwsp.chapter3.drawing.data.DrawingAsIterator;
```

```java
import jwsp.chapter3.drawing.data.DrawingFromReader;
import jwsp.chapter3.drawing.data.DrawingObject;

@ServerEndpoint("/draw")
public class DrawingServer {
    private Session session;

    @OnOpen
    public void initSession(Session session) {
        this.session = session;
    }

    @OnMessage
    public void shapeCreated(Reader reader) {
        DrawingObject drawingObject;
        try (Reader rdr = reader) {
            DrawingFromReader dp = new DrawingFromReader(rdr);
            drawingObject = dp.getDrawingObject();

        } catch (IOException e) {
            System.out.println("There was an error reading the
                                        incoming message.");
            return;
        }
        DrawingObject toSend = new DrawingObject(
                            drawingObject.getShape(),
                            drawingObject.getCenter(),
                            drawingObject.getRadius(),
                        this.getFadedColor(drawingObject.getColor()));
        for (Session otherSession : this.session.getOpenSessions()) {
            if (!otherSession.equals(this.session)) {
                try {
                    DrawingAsIterator dai = new DrawingAsIterator(toSend);
                    sendDrawing(otherSession, dai);
                } catch (IOException ioe) {
                    System.out.println("Communication error: " +
                                                ioe.getMessage());
                }
            }
        }
    }

    private Color getFadedColor(Color c) {
        Color faded = new Color((int) 255 - ((255-c.getRed()) / 2),
                        (int) 255 - ((255-c.getGreen()) / 2),
                        (int) 255 - ((255-c.getBlue()) / 2));
        return faded;
    }

    @OnError
    public void handleError(Throwable thw) {
        if (thw instanceof DecodeException) {
            System.out.println("Error decoding incoming message: " +
                                ((DecodeException)thw).getText());
```

```
            } else {
                System.out.println("Server WebSocket error: " +
                                                thw.getMessage());
            }
        }

        private void sendDrawing(Session aSession,
                        Iterator<String> drawingAsIterator)
                                        throws IOException {
            RemoteEndpoint.Basic remote = aSession.getBasicRemote();
            while (drawingAsIterator.hasNext()) {
                String partialMessage = drawingAsIterator.next();
                boolean isLast = !drawingAsIterator.hasNext();
                remote.sendText(partialMessage, isLast);
            }
        }

}
```

The purpose of the DrawingServer is to handle messages coming in from connected clients representing the DrawingObjects they are adding to their canvases. Each time a connected client sends such a message, in the form of a DrawingObject encoded by the DrawingEncoder, the DrawingServer endpoint processes the message in its shapeCreated() method. You will notice on the DrawingServer that we are not using any Java WebSocket encoders or decoders to manage the messages. Instead, in order to illustrate some of the other modes of processing messages we talked about earlier in this chapter, we have chosen to process messages in the form of a java.io.Reader, the parameter type to this shapeCreated() method, and to send messages using the form devoted to sending a WebSocket message in the form of a sequence of partial text messages. You will notice that the shapeCreated() implementation uses a support class, the DrawingFromReader class, to read from the reader and formulate the DrawingObject instance from the data read. It uses the same representation of the DrawingObject as a character stream that the DrawingDecoder does, as you can see here:

**Listing:**    *The DrawingFromReader Class*

```
import java.awt.Color;
import java.awt.Point;
import java.io.*;
import java.util.*;

public class DrawingFromReader {
    private Reader reader;

    public DrawingFromReader(Reader r) throws IOException {
        this.reader = r;
    }
```

```java
public DrawingObject getDrawingObject() {
    Iterator<String> readerItr = new
                    DrawingObjectReaderIterator(this.reader);
    String message_name = readerItr.next();
    Shape shape = Shape.fromString(readerItr.next());
    Point center = new Point(new Integer(readerItr.next()),
                            new Integer(readerItr.next()));
    int radius = new Integer(readerItr.next());
    Color color = new Color(new Integer(readerItr.next()));
    return new DrawingObject(shape, center, radius, color);
}

class DrawingObjectReaderIterator implements Iterator<String> {
    private Reader reader;
    private boolean hasNext;

    DrawingObjectReaderIterator(Reader reader) {
        this.reader = reader;
    }

    @Override
    public boolean hasNext() {
        return hasNext;
    }

    @Override
    public String next() {
        try {
            StringBuilder sb = new StringBuilder();
            int i = 0;
            while ( (i=reader.read()) != -1 ) {
                if ((char) i == ',') {
                    break;
                } else {
                    sb.append((char) i);
                }
            }
            if (i == -1) {
                this.hasNext = false;
            }
            String s = sb.toString();
            return s;
        } catch (IOException ioe) {
            throw new RuntimeException("Error parsing from reader");
        }
    }

    @Override
    public void remove() {
        throw new UnsupportedOperationException();
    }
}

}
```

Then the `DrawingServer`'s `shapeCreated()` method goes on to use what is sometimes referred to as the broadcast method on the `Session` object method:

```
public Set<Session> getOpenSessions()
```

which returns the set of all the open sessions. As a reminder, each client that is connected to this server endpoint is associated with a unique WebSocket connection, each of which in turn is represented by a unique `Session` instance. So this method is a very convenient way of listing all the connected clients to this endpoint. The method tweaks the color property of the shape and broadcasts the new shape to each of the connected clients except the one that sent the update. The update to each client is delegated to the `sendDrawing()` method. This method uses the support class `DrawingAsIterator`, which converts the `DrawingObject` into an iterator of `String` objects representing the properties of the `DrawingObject`. The `DrawingAsIterator` class uses the same representation as the `DrawingEncoder` for conversion, as you can see in the following code:

**Listing:**   *The `DrawingAsIterator` Class*

```java
import java.util.Iterator;

public class DrawingAsIterator implements Iterator<String> {
    private DrawingObject drawingObject;
    private int index = 0;

    public DrawingAsIterator(DrawingObject drawingObject) {
        this.drawingObject = drawingObject;
    }

    @Override
    public String next() {
        index++;
        switch (index) {
            case 1:
                return DrawingObject.MESSAGE_NAME;
            case 2:
                return ",";
            case 3:
                return drawingObject.getShape().toString();
            case 4:
                return ",";
            case 5:
                return Integer.toString(drawingObject.getCenter().x);
            case 6:
                return ",";
```

```
        case 7:
            return Integer.toString(drawingObject.getCenter().y);
        case 8:
            return ",";
        case 9:
            return Integer.toString(drawingObject.getRadius());
        case 10:
            return ",";
        case 11:
            return Integer.toString(drawingObject.getColor().getRGB());
        default:
            throw new IllegalStateException("No more elements");
        }
    }

    @Override
    public boolean hasNext() {
        return this.index < 11;
    }

    @Override
    public void remove() {
        throw new UnsupportedOperationException();
    }
}
```

The DrawingServer's sendDrawing() method uses the Java WebSocket
API RemoteEndpoint.Basic's

```
public void sendText(String partialString, boolean isLast)
                                            throws IOException
```

method to send each piece of the DrawingObject's string representation
out to the connected client. In this way, the DrawingServer keeps all its
connected clients up-to-date with the contents of the group drawing canvas.

Let's step back for a moment and think about what we are seeing in this
example. On the client side, you can see that we have utilized the encoder
and decoder mechanisms of the Java WebSocket API to handle the WebSocket
message formats. This means that the DrawingClient endpoint only ever
needs to deal with DrawingObject instances and never needs to know the
representation of the DrawingObjects as WebSocket messages. This work is
delegated to the encoder and decoder it uses.

On the server side, the DrawingServer, whose job it is to listen for
changes on any of its connected clients and broadcast the update to all the
others, does deal with the DrawingObjects in raw WebSocket message
form—on the incoming side, as a character stream it has to parse, and on

the outgoing side, as a collection of strings it sends in a sequence of partial messages back to the client it is updating.

Even though the `DrawingServer` endpoint sends the drawing updates as sequences of partial strings, the client needs the whole message in order to interpret it as a drawing update, so the WebSocket implementation is buffering the incoming message until all of it has been received. Only then does it make its call to the `DrawingDecoder` in order to convert it into a `DrawingObject` representing the drawing update.

We included a range of message processing choices in the DrawingBoard application in order to illustrate some of the options we laid out at the beginning of the chapter. In a real world application, you would probably choose only one or two of those options. In fact, in the interest of simplicity and short code, you might be tempted to refactor the `DrawingServer` endpoint to use the `DrawingEncoder` and `DrawingDecoder` even before you finish reading the chapter!

# Messaging and Threading

Before we conclude this chapter, we turn to a very important topic for Java developers: threading. You can easily see in the drawing example that as you increase the number of clients you increase the chances that two clients will simultaneously update the server at the same time. This will also increase the chances that a client will send an update at the same time the server is in the middle of updating some of the other clients. What guarantees do you have as a WebSocket developer about how many threads will call your endpoint at the same time, and what guarantees do you have, particularly if a WebSocket message is being sent as a sequence of partial messages, that the messages will arrive in the order you sent them and won't get mixed up with other messages?

## WebSocket Endpoint Threading and Messaging

Fortunately, for developers, Java WebSocket API provides a number of simple assurances that answer these questions:

- The Java WebSocket API creates a new instance of a server endpoint each time a new client connects.

- Each WebSocket endpoint instance is only ever called by one thread at a time.

■ When a WebSocket message arrives in parts, the Java WebSocket API must ensure that the corresponding endpoint is called in the correct order and that the message parts do not interleave with other messages.

These three assurances guarantee a straightforward single-threaded model for endpoints and rules out some of the unfortunate situations described above. This also means that each endpoint instance only ever sees the same single session instance representing the unique client connection that caused its creation. The session can be held as an instance variable, as it is in the DrawingServer endpoint.

# Threading and Lifecycle of Encoders and Decoders

For developers of Encoder and Decoder classes, the Java WebSocket API guarantees that one instance of the Encoder or Decoder class is created per WebSocket connection. Together with the assurances during message processing outlined above, this means, for example, that developers of decoders can expect no more than one thread to be in the decode() method at a time, removing the need to develop code defensively for concurrent access to the method. The init() method of Encoder and Decoder instances are called after the connection to which they are attached has been established but before the first message that will need them needs processing. The destroy() method of Encoder and Decoder instances are called as the connection is closing.

One question that does come to mind, especially for developers of WebSocket applications on the server side, is where can application state be held that is common to all the client connections? We might easily want to extend the DrawingBoard application to retain the drawings that multiple clients collaborate on, or we might want a new client joining the group to be updated with the complete group drawing created up to the point at which it joined. Since there is a new server endpoint instance for each new client, we cannot hold the group drawing there. We will return to the topic of endpoint state in Chapter 4 as we examine more closely the properties and uses of the Session object.

# Summary

In this chapter, we examined closely all the means by which you can receive WebSocket messages using the Java WebSocket API. This included the various representations of WebSocket text, binary, and pong messages as Java objects, and included a breakdown of how to use the @OnMessage annotation and when to implement the various MessageHandler interfaces. We examined the synchronous modes for sending WebSocket messages of various forms using the RemoteEndpoint.Basic APIs. We covered the built-in encoding/decoding schemes in the Java WebSocket API. Finally, we illustrated many of these concepts by walking through the DrawingBoard sample.

# CHAPTER

## 4

# Configurations and Sessions

I n this chapter, we will examine two of the most important objects in the Java WebSocket API: the `Session` and the `EndpointConfig`. These objects inside a running WebSocket application represent the configuration information of an endpoint and the active connection to a peer, respectively. They are the foundations in which developers can build application state. We will start right out with the Chat sample. The Chat sample is a simple JavaScript client to the Java WebSocket server application that makes use of several features of `Session` and `EndpointConfig` and paves the way for a more detailed exposition of the utilities of these APIs.

# Session State and Logical Endpoint State

We arrived at this chapter through a discussion of the Group Drawing sample. The users of this application collaborated on a group drawing. However, as you probably realized, in the application the group drawing didn't actually exist anywhere except as a series of drawing updates over a period of time in which the users were connected. Most web applications of any importance generate some form of information or effect that is longer lived than the application itself: a drawing collaboration between multiple users that results in a reproducible drawing to show others, a sequence of guest comments that over time forms a community critique of a restaurant, a number of customer addresses that results in a route to follow on a pizza delivery map, a series of messages that results in a permanent record of a conversation, and so on. This leads us to the following question:

Where in a WebSocket application can we hold application state that is common to all the connected clients? Where in our drawing application could we hold the collective drawing?

Now, the Java Enterprise Edition (Java EE) developer has many options for holding application state, but they are all dependent on understanding where to pull application state from the Java WebSocket application.

Inherent in a multiple client, single-server model are the following two application states: state associated with a single connected peer and state associated with all of the connected peers. Imagine a pizza delivery application where customers can enter their orders and their addresses. At periodic intervals, the pizza delivery team can ask the application to generate a listing of orders and a delivery map for the orders. Each order and address is application state associated with a single client, whereas the order list and delivery map is application state associated with many clients. Imagine the group drawing application. Each drawing shape is application state that is associated with the client that drew it, whereas the final picture is application state associated with all the clients that collaborated on it.

The Chat sample is one of the best ways to illustrate these two kinds of application states and will lead us directly into the two objects of this chapter: the `Session`, which represents per-client state, and the `EndpointConfig`, which correlates with the state of the endpoint shared with multiple clients.

# The Chat Sample

There are many variants on a chat application. Some allow only group chatting, wherein all the chat messages are visible to everyone. Other chat applications list everyone who is available to chat, but only allow private, one-to-one conversations. And many chat applications allow both group and private modes of communication.

Our chat example is a group chat example, where there is a common chat transcript that holds the chat messages from all the users who have signed on. This is the application state that builds up during the course of running the Chat application that is common to all the connected users. The application state that is common only to one connected user in this application is the username. The Chat sample uses a JavaScript client which connects to a WebSocket server endpoint. Up to now, we have listed all the sample application code. For this sample, and for some of the samples that follow in the rest of the book, we will limit our code listing to the most relevant pieces pertaining to the things we are learning about the Java WebSocket API.

To begin, take a look at screenshots of the Chat sample running, first as the user signs in (see Figure 4-1), and then as the Chat sample gets more active with several users and a long chat transcript (see Figure 4-2).

**FIGURE 4-1.** *Signing in to the Chat sample*

Before we look at the code, following is a quick overview of the message interactions, as shown in Figure 4-3. After a WebSocket connection has been established between the client and the server, we can see from the figure that the Chat conversation begins with the chat client sending a sign-in request message. This message contains a proposed username that the client would like to use. The chat server responds immediately with a confirmed name that the client may use during chat. This ensures that the server is able to pick a unique name for the client joining in the chat conversation. Pretty clearly, chat applications allowing two clients to use the same username would quickly get confusing!

Each time a new user signs in, the chat server issues a message to all connected clients containing the most current list of users that are signed into the Chat sample. Each time the user types a new message into the chat

**FIGURE 4-2.**   *The active Chat window*

window, the chat client sends a chat message to the server. The server adds this message, together with the username of the client that sent it, to the chat transcript that holds a record of all the chat messages sent by all the clients of the Chat sample. Whenever the chat server does so, it issues a transcript update message to all the clients that are currently connected so that they may display the new message that one of the chat users added. When the user has said all he or she has to say, the sign-out process is such that the chat client sends a sign-out request to the chat server, which updates the remaining users with a transcript update message to say that the user is signing out, and then closes the WebSocket connection.

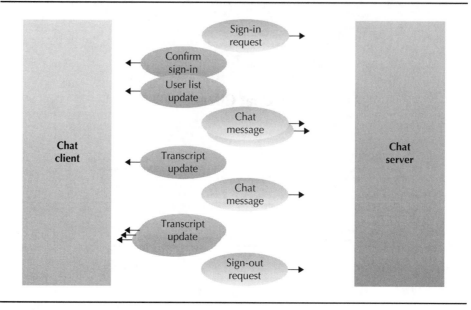

**FIGURE 4-3.** *Chat messaging interactions*

Now that we have understood the message choreography of the Chat sample, let's take a look at the heart of the Chat sample, which is the `ChatServer` endpoint:

**Listing:** *ChatServer Endpoint*

```java
import java.io.IOException;
import java.util.*;
import javax.websocket.*;
import javax.websocket.server.*;
import jwsp.chapter4.data.*;

@ServerEndpoint(value = "/chat-server",
        subprotocols={"chat"},
        decoders = {ChatDecoder.class},
        encoders = {ChatEncoder.class},
        configurator=ChatServerConfigurator.class)
public class ChatServer {
    private static String USERNAME_KEY = "username";
    private static String USERNAMES_KEY = "usernames";

    private Session session;
    private ServerEndpointConfig endpointConfig;
    private Transcript transcript;
```

```java
@OnOpen
public void startChatChannel(EndpointConfig config, Session session) {
    this.endpointConfig = (ServerEndpointConfig) config;
    ChatServerConfigurator csc =
      (ChatServerConfigurator) endpointConfig.getConfigurator();
    this.transcript = csc.getTranscript();
    this.session = session;
}

@OnMessage
public void handleChatMessage(ChatMessage message) {
    switch (message.getType()){
        case NewUserMessage.USERNAME_MESSAGE:
            this.processNewUser((NewUserMessage) message);
            break;
        case ChatMessage.CHAT_DATA_MESSAGE:
            this.processChatUpdate((ChatUpdateMessage) message);
            break;
        case ChatMessage.SIGNOFF_REQUEST:
            this.processSignoffRequest((UserSignoffMessage) message);
    }
}

@OnError
public void myError(Throwable t) {
    System.out.println("Error: " + t.getMessage());
}

@OnClose
public void endChatChannel() {
    if (this.getCurrentUsername() != null) {
        this.addMessage(" just left...without even signing out !");
        this.removeUser();
    }
}

void processNewUser(NewUserMessage message) {
    String newUsername = this.validateUsername(message.getUsername());
    NewUserMessage uMessage = new NewUserMessage(newUsername);
    try {
        session.getBasicRemote().sendObject(uMessage);
    } catch (IOException | EncodeException ioe) {
        System.out.println("Error signing " + message.getUsername()
                                    + " into chat : " + ioe.getMessage());
    }
    this.registerUser(newUsername);
    this.broadcastUserListUpdate();
    this.addMessage(" just joined.");
}

void processChatUpdate(ChatUpdateMessage message) {
    this.addMessage(message.getMessage());
}

void processSignoffRequest(UserSignoffMessage drm) {
    this.addMessage(" just left.");
```

```java
        this.removeUser();
    }

    private String getCurrentUsername() {
        return (String) session.getUserProperties().get(USERNAME_KEY);
    }

    private void registerUser(String username) {
        session.getUserProperties().put(USERNAME_KEY, username);
        this.updateUserList();
    }

    private void updateUserList() {
        List<String> usernames = new ArrayList<>();
        for (Session s : session.getOpenSessions()) {
            String uname = (String) s.getUserProperties().get(USERNAME_KEY);
            usernames.add(uname);
        }
        this.endpointConfig.getUserProperties().put(USERNAMES_KEY,
                                                    usernames);
    }

    private List<String> getUserList() {
        List<String> userList =
            (List<String>) this.endpointConfig.getUserProperties().
                get(USERNAMES_KEY);
        return (userList == null) ? new ArrayList<String>() : userList;
    }


    private String validateUsername(String newUsername) {
        if (this.getUserList().contains(newUsername)) {
            return this.validateUsername(newUsername + "1");
        }
        return newUsername;
    }

    private void broadcastUserListUpdate() {
        UserListUpdateMessage ulum =
          new UserListUpdateMessage(this.getUserList());
        for (Session nextSession : session.getOpenSessions()) {
            try {
                nextSession.getBasicRemote().sendObject(ulum);
            } catch (IOException | EncodeException ex) {
                System.out.println("Error updating a client : "
                                            + ex.getMessage());
            }
        }
    }

    private void removeUser() {
        try {
            this.updateUserList();
            this.broadcastUserListUpdate();
            this.session.getUserProperties().remove(USERNAME_KEY);
            this.session.close(new CloseReason(
                CloseReason.CloseCodes.NORMAL_CLOSURE,
                "User logged off"));
```

```
        } catch (IOException e) {
            System.out.println("Error removing user");
        }
    }

    private void broadcastTranscriptUpdate() {
        for (Session nextSession : session.getOpenSessions()) {
            ChatUpdateMessage cdm = new ChatUpdateMessage(
                            this.transcript.getLastUsername(),
                            this.transcript.getLastMessage());
            try {
                nextSession.getBasicRemote().sendObject(cdm);
            } catch (IOException | EncodeException ex) {
                System.out.println("Error updating a client : "
                                        + ex.getMessage());
            }
        }
    }

    private void addMessage(String message) {
        this.transcript.addEntry(this.getCurrentUsername(), message);
        this.broadcastTranscriptUpdate();
    }

}
```

Let's start our survey of this endpoint by looking at the data it holds via its instance variables. It holds a reference to the session instance. You will remember that, because there is one instance of each server endpoint per client connection, this reference the ChatServer instance holds is to the unique Session instance associated with the client connection.

The ChatServer could equally ask for this Session instance to be passed into all of its lifecycle methods, the session is always an optional parameter of the @OnOpen, @OnMessage, @OnError, and @OnClose annotated methods, but since some of the application logic of the ChatServer is factored into separate methods, it is a little more convenient to be able to reference the session as an instance variable rather than always having to pass it around into various method calls. Many endpoints do not have a design choice about this; those that need to send a message that is not in response to an incoming message have to maintain a reference to the Session object so they can access the RemoteEndpoint to send the message. The second piece of data the ChatServer uses is the ServerEndpointConfig object. You will remember we created a ServerEndpointConfig when we deployed a programmatic endpoint in Chapter 1. EndpointConfig objects hold all the configuration data and algorithms needed to configure a WebSocket endpoint. We will discuss them in some detail shortly, but for now we will note that the `ServerEndpointConfig` contains all the configuration information held in the class-level `@ServerEndpoint` annotation used by the `ChatServer` endpoint. It also has the very useful property that the WebSocket implementation will create precisely one `ServerEndpointConfig` instance for all instances of the `ChatServer` endpoint. This means that the `ServerEndpointConfig` is an extremely useful place to hold data that is common to all clients of the `ChatServer` endpoint. In other words, it is a great place to store the list of currently signed-in users of the Chat application, and it's a great place to store the chat transcript. Relying on this cardinality of the `ServerEndpointConfig` in the Chat application, two different approaches have been used to store these "global" pieces of application state. First, you will see that the list of currently signed-in users is stored in the property map available on the `ServerEndpointConfig`. Second, you will notice from the `@ServerEndpoint` annotation definition that it defines a class in the configurator attribute called the `ChatServerConfigurator` class, which holds onto the other piece of global application state: the chat transcript. Let's look briefly at this configurator class.

**Listing:** *ChatServerConfigurator Class*

```
import javax.websocket.HandshakeResponse;
import javax.websocket.server.HandshakeRequest;
import javax.websocket.server.ServerEndpointConfig;

public class ChatServerConfigurator
extends ServerEndpointConfig.Configurator {
    private Transcript transcript;

    public ChatServerConfigurator() {
        this.transcript = new Transcript(20);
    }

    public Transcript getTranscript() {
        return this.transcript;
    }

    @Override
    public void modifyHandshake(ServerEndpointConfig sec,
                                    HandshakeRequest request,
                                    HandshakeResponse response) {
        System.out.println("Handshake Request headers: "
                                + request.getHeaders());
        System.out.println("Handshake Response headers: "
                                + response.getHeaders());
    }
}
```

In overriding the `ServerEndpointConfig.Configurator`, this class is able to intercept configuration callbacks from the WebSocket implementation. This class has chosen to intercept the opening handshake HTTP request and HTTP response in order to simply log the headers. This class stores the chat transcript as we mentioned above, modeled by the `Transcript` class:

**Listing:**   *Transcript Class*

```java
import java.util.ArrayList;
import java.util.List;

public class Transcript {
    private List<String> messages = new ArrayList<>();
    private List<String> usernames = new ArrayList<>();
    private int maxLines;

    Transcript(int maxLines) {
        this.maxLines = maxLines;
    }

    public String getLastUsername() {
        return usernames.get(usernames.size() -1);
    }

    public String getLastMessage() {
        return messages.get(messages.size() -1);
    }

    public void addEntry(String username, String message) {
        if (usernames.size() > maxLines) {
            usernames.remove(0);
            messages.remove(0);
        }
        usernames.add(username);
        messages.add(message);
    }
}
```

Because the WebSocket implementation instantiates one `ServerEndpointConfig` instance for all the `ChatServer` endpoint instances, the single transcript referenced by the `ServerEndpointConfig`'s configurator is the single transcript shared by all the `ChatServer` endpoint instances.

Returning to the code listing for the `ChatServer`, you will notice that the `ChatServer` obtains its reference to the transcript via the `ServerEndpointConfig`. This ensures that chat messages from all the users are written to the same global transcript.

You will notice that these instance variables are set up when the WebSocket connection is established in the `startChatChannel()` method, marked with the `@OnOpen` annotation.

Notice also that the `ChatServer` never deals directly with the native text or binary formats of WebSocket messages. Instead, it has configured both an `Encoder` implementation and a `Decoder` implementation to mean that it only ever sends instances of the `ChatMessage` class and only ever receives messages in the form of a `ChatMessage` class coming into the `handleChatMessage()` method, duly annotated with the `@OnMessage` annotation.

You will also see that the username of the currently signed-in user is held in the property map on the `Session` object. You might also notice that there are two ways for a user to leave the conversation in this application: one is a nice way, and one is rather rude! If the user presses the Sign Out button, the client, as we mentioned above, issues a sign-out request to the chat server. The chat server in turn removes the username from the current session and broadcasts the change in the user list and the added farewell message to all the other connected clients. Only then does it close the WebSocket connection. If, however, the user navigates away from the client page or closes the browser window, the client code simply closes the WebSocket connection. In this case, the `ChatServer` endpoint experiences this exit from the chat conversation when its `endChatConversation()`, annotated with the `@OnClose` method, is called. In this case, it removes the user and notifies the other signed-in users, but with a less polite message.

You will also notice in the `@ServerEndpoint` annotation the subprotocol attribute, with a list containing the string `chat`. WebSocket subprotocols are a very lightweight way to define that an endpoint expects to use a specific format and choreography of WebSocket messages to function properly. In this sample, we have decided to call the particular collection of chat messages and the specific order they must be sent the "chat" subprotocol, and we have declared that the `ChatServer` endpoint uses this subprotocol. You will also notice that the JavaScript client declares this subprotocol when it creates its WebSocket connection to the `EchoServer`. What we call the "chat" protocol here is entirely specific to the Chat application, and it is simply a useful way of flagging that both the client and server pieces of the application have agreed on a common message format and choreography. We will learn more about WebSocket subprotocols shortly.

The following points recap the main takeaways from this Chat sample. The sample:

- Uses custom encoders and decoders to send and receive messages

- Stores user-specific state (the username) in the `Session` object associated with the `ChatServer` instance

- Stores application state common to all users (signed in user list and chat transcript) using two different attributes of the `ServerEndpointConfig` object: the property map it holds and a custom `ServerEndpointConfig.Configurator`

- Defines a WebSocket subprotocol called `chat` that it uses to flag the specific message formats and choreography it uses

**NOTE**

*When designing where to hold application state common to all users in your application, you have a choice whether to use the property map on the `ServerEndpointConfig` or whether to implement your own `ServletEndpointConfig` `.Configurator`. Both approaches are valid. In general, for single immutable objects, the property approach is lighter weight because it doesn't require the creation of a new class; but if the application data is more complicated and you need to perform calculations on it or if you want more type safety, you should consider extending the `ServletEndpointConfig.Configurator`.*

Feel free to examine the rest of the code in this application. Next, we will turn to a more formal examination of the `EndpointConfig` and `Session` objects that are so central to this pivotal sample.

# Configuring Endpoints: ClientEndpointConfig and ServerEndpointConfig

In this section, we will examine in some detail the various configuration options that are available to developers of all kinds of WebSocket endpoints, whether they are deployed on a server, whether they are intended as part of a client application, or whether they are programmatic or annotated endpoints.

## Supplying and Accessing Endpoint Configuration Information

In the Java WebSocket API, WebSocket endpoints are configured using information and algorithms that are modeled in `EndpointConfig` classes. Server-side endpoints are configured with the information held in the API's `ServerEndpointConfig` class, and client-side endpoints are configured with the information held in its `ClientEndpointConfig` class.

If you only ever use annotated endpoints, you will see that you supply the configuration information using the `@ClientEndpoint` or the `@ServerEndpoint` annotations. The WebSocket information uses the information held in these annotations to create the instances of `ClientEndpointConfig` or `ServerEndpointConfig`, respectively, that are used at deployment time to configure each endpoint instance and that are available as optional parameters to the lifecycle methods.

If you only ever use programmatic endpoints, you will know that you supply the configuration information for your endpoints by constructing instances of the appropriate `EndpointConfig` by using either the `ClientEndpointConfig` `.Builder` class or the `ServerEndpointConfig.Builder` class. In the case of server-side endpoints, you supply the `ServerEndpointConfig` instance you want to use in the `ServerApplicationConfig` implementation you provide with your programmatic server endpoint. We saw this, for example, in Chapter 1 when deploying the ProgrammaticEcho sample. In the case of client-side endpoints, you supply the `ClientEndpointConfig` instance you want to use to the relevant `WebSocketContainer.connectToServer()` method that you use to deploy the endpoint. Just as with annotated endpoints, the `EndpointConfig` that the WebSocket implementation uses to construct your endpoint instances is available from each of those endpoint instances via the

```
public abstract void onOpen(Session session, EndpointConfig config)
```

method you had to implement when you subclassed the programmatic `Endpoint` class.

**NOTE**
*In all cases, when the endpoint is deployed,
there is precisely one EndpointConfig instance
holding the configuration information for all the
instances of the endpoint class.*

Before we move on to examine the `EndpointConfig` classes in more detail, we summarize the different configurations in the following table.

| Endpoint Type | Configuration Information Supplied | EndpointConfig Available |
|---|---|---|
| Programmatic server | By constructing a `ServerEndpointConfig` in the supplied `ServerApplicationConfig` | In the `Endpoint` `.onOpen()` method |
| Annotated server | Declared in `@ServerEndpoint` | As an optional parameter to the endpoint lifecycle methods |
| Programmatic client | By constructing a `ClientEndpointConfig` needed by the `WebSocketContainer` `.connectToServer()` method | In the `Endpoint` `.onOpen()` method |
| Annotated client | Declared in `@ClientEndpoint` | As an optional parameter to the endpoint lifecycle methods |

# Examining the Configuration Options

Common to all endpoint configurations, whether the endpoints are intended for the client or the server side, are the following properties:

- A list of encoders, available at runtime via `EndpointConfig.getEncoders()`

- A list of decoders, available at runtime via `EndpointConfig.getDecoders()`

- A property map for developer objects, available at runtime via `EndpointConfig.getUserProperties()`

Here is a table that summarizes how the configuration properties common to both client- and server-side endpoints are added to the endpoint definition:

| Configuration Property | Annotated Endpoint | Programmatic Endpoints |
|---|---|---|
| Encoders list | `encoders()` attribute on `@ServerEndpoint` or `@ClientEndpoint` | `ClientEndpointConfig.Builder`<br>  `.encoders(`<br>    `List<Class<? extends Encoder>> encoders)`<br>or<br>`ServerEndpointConfig.Builder`<br>  `.encoders(`<br>    `List<Class<? extends Encoder>> encoders)` |
| Decoders list | `decoders()` attribute on `@ServerEndpoint` or `@ClientEndpoint` | `ClientEndpointConfig`<br>  `.Builder.decoders(`<br>    `List<Class<? extends Decoder>> decoders)`<br>or<br>`ServerEndpointConfig`<br>  `.Builder.decoders(`<br>    `List<Class<? extends Decoder>> decoders)` |
| Developer object map | `EndpointConfig`<br>  `.getUserProperties()` | `EndpointConfig.getUserProperties()` |

The encoders list is a list of Java classes that implement one of the `Encoder` interfaces that you would like to be used to encode your developer objects when sending objects that are not one of the standard types that the Java WebSocket API will handle automatically. As a reminder, those types are `String`, `byte[]`, `ByteBuffer`, or Java primitives and class equivalents.

You may have different Java objects in your application that you would like to send to a peer. In this case, you may need to provide multiple encoders. In such cases, the Java WebSocket implementation will select the first `Encoder` in the list that can encode the object you are trying to send. For example, if you had two encoders for your `Banana` class, one that implemented `Encoder.Text<Banana>` and one that implemented `Encoder.Binary<Banana>`, your application would send `Banana`s in either text form or binary form, depending on whether the encoder implementing `Encoder.Text<Banana>` was before the encoder implementing `Encoder.Binary<Banana>`, or the other way, in the encoders list you supplied in the WebSocket annotation or on the `EndpointConfig` you constructed.

The decoders list is a list of Java classes that implement one of the `Decoder` interfaces. When a WebSocket message arrives for processing by the endpoint, the WebSocket implementation uses the first `Decoder` class that declares it can deal with the native type (text or binary) of the message and that returns true from its `willDecode()` method. For example, if your application has elected to receive `Banana` objects and you have configured some `Decoder` classes that can decode WebSocket messages into `Banana` instances, if a binary message arrives, the WebSocket implementation will look for the first `Decoder` in the list that can decode binary WebSocket messages into `Banana` instances (that is to say, classes that implement either `Decoder.Binary<Banana>` or `Decoder.BinaryStream<Banana>`). If the `Decoder` is a `Decoder.Binary<Banana>`, the implementation will perform the additional check to see that the `Decoder`'s `willDecode()` method returns `true` before either using it if it does or looking further down the `Decoder` list if not.

The developer object map is an editable `java.util.Map` with `String` keys and `Object` values that developers may use to store any application state that is common to all instances of the endpoint this configuration object is configuring. As we saw in the Chat sample, this developer object map was a great place to store and maintain the list of currently signed-in users of the Chat application.

Before we look at the various other client- and server-side configuration properties for WebSocket endpoints, we'll take a small diversion into a pair of mechanisms built into the WebSocket network protocol that we will need to understand first.

# WebSocket Subprotocols and WebSocket Extensions

Even in a relatively simple application such as a chat application, we saw earlier in this chapter that it defines a particular format for the text messages it uses for its client/server communication, and it also defines a particular sequencing or choreography of message interactions. In fact, all WebSocket applications will define some sort of application-specific message formats and some sort of application-specific choreography. The WebSocket protocol uses the name WebSocket *subprotocols* for these application-specific formats and choreographies that build on top of the raw WebSocket message formats and connection lifecycle. A WebSocket subprotocol is marked by a simple string name. In our Chat example, we defined our particular choreography of chat messages to be the "chat" subprotocol. It may turn out that some standard WebSocket protocols will emerge, in which case you should be careful when thinking up subprotocol names for your application, but while there is a WebSocket subprotocol registry at www.iana.org, it seems that the subprotocol name is being used mostly as a simple way to mark applications with a concise moniker to encapsulate its particular conversational conventions.

At a deeper level, the WebSocket protocol allows for arbitrary data to be inserted within the data frames that it uses to communicate events and data between endpoints. This data may be used to route the frames through intermediate servers carrying the connection or may be used to describe or qualify the WebSocket data held within the data frame. If a WebSocket implementation decided to use this facility of the protocol, in so doing it would actually be extending the WebSocket protocol, and such schemes are called WebSocket *extensions*.

WebSocket extensions are known by a string name and a collection of name-value pairs that configure the extension. A small number of extensions have been formally proposed, such as an extension called DEFLATE, which allows compressed data to be carried in a WebSocket message to improve transmission efficiency, and the MUX extension that allows multiple logical WebSocket connections to run over one physical TCP connection to improve network scalability. As WebSockets get ever more popular, the number of subprotocols and extensions is sure to rise.

## Client-Side-Only Configuration Properties

Client-side endpoints are able to specify the following configuration properties:

- A list of WebSocket subprotocol names, available at runtime via `ClientEndpointConfig.getPreferredSubprotocols()`

- A list of WebSocket extensions, available at runtime via `ClientEndpointConfig.getExtensions()`

- The `ClientEndpoint.Configurator` class, available at runtime via `ClientEndpointConfig.getConfigurator()`

The list of WebSocket subprotocol names is a list of `String` names you can provide as part of the configuration. The list is used during the opening handshake, that is, when the WebSocket connection is being established with the server to negotiate the subprotocol that both sides will agree to use. The list of extensions is a list of `javax.websocket.Extension` objects, each of which encapsulates the name and a list of extension properties that describe a WebSocket extension. You can use this property to specify all the extensions you would like to use when this client endpoint connects to a server, and the order in which the extensions should be applied to the WebSocket protocol used for the connection. Just like for subprotocols, during the opening handshake of the WebSocket connection there is a negotiation that takes place so that both ends of the WebSocket connection agree on the WebSocket extensions they will use for the connection being established. The WebSocket extensions available in the WebSocket implementation you are using can be listed on the `WebSocketContainer` using the `getInstalledExtensions()` call.

When we look in more detail at the configuration of server endpoints, the more we will be able understand more about how the negotiations of WebSocket subprotocols and WebSocket extensions work and can be customized.

The `ClientEndpointConfig.Configurator` class is a class that can be used to intercept the actual HTTP request and response that the underlying WebSocket implementation formulates and receives back from the WebSocket server. If you do not provide one explicitly, the WebSocket implementation will provide one for you. This class has two methods. The

```
public void beforeRequest(Map<String,List<String>> headers)
```

method is called after the WebSocket implementation has formulated the opening handshake request it wants to send in order to initiate the connection.

The headers that are passed into this method can be added to or can be altered if you decide to supply your own `Configurator` implementation. The

```
public void afterResponse(HandshakeResponse hr)
```

method is called after the WebSocket implementation has received the opening handshake response from the WebSocket server. The `HandshakeResponse` may be examined and its headers interrogated.

The most common use cases for providing a custom `ClientEndpointConfig.Configurator` to configure a client endpoint revolve around inserting custom HTTP headers in the opening handshake request or editing them, such as inserting or updating an HTTP cookie or authentication information and reading back cookies or authentication challenges from the server. This is a more advanced use of the Java WebSocket API, and many developers will not need to use this facility.

It is possible, however, to subclass the `ClientEndpointConfig` `.Configurator` to add any number of application- or framework-specific features, such as access to a database or remote web service that you would like to be available to your endpoint. In fact, you can use the same `ClientEndpointConfig.Configurator` instance to configure a number of different client endpoints so that multiple client endpoints can all share the same services, such as a database connection. This makes the configurator a very flexible way to introduce other services or features into your client WebSocket application.

We'll end this section with a summary of how the client-side-only configuration property endpoints are added to the endpoint definition.

| Configuration Property | Annotated Endpoint | Programmatic Endpoint |
|---|---|---|
| Subprotocols | `subprotocols()` attribute on `@ClientEndpoint` | `ClientEndpointConfig.Builder` `.preferredSubprotocols(` `List<String> subprotocols)` |
| Extensions | `extensions()` attribute on `@ClientEndpoint` | `ClientEndpointConfig.Builder` `.extensions(` `List<Extension> extensions)` |
| Configurator | `configurator()` attribute on `@ClientEndpoint` | `ClientEndpointConfig.Builder` `.configurator(ClientEndpointConfig` `.Configurator configurator)` |

## Server-Side-Only Configuration Properties

Server-side endpoints are configured with the following properties:

- The endpoint path, available at runtime using the `ServerEndpointConfig.getPath()` call

- The endpoint class, available at runtime using the `ServerEndpointConfig.getEndpointClass()` call

- The subprotocols supported by the endpoint, available at runtime using the `ServerEndpointConfig.getSubprotocols()` call

- The extensions supported by the endpoint, available at runtime using the `ServerEndpointConfig.getExtensions()` call

- The `ServerEndpointConfig.Configurator`, available at runtime using the `ServerEndpointConfig.getConfigurator()` call

This is the path, relative to the context root of the web application holding the endpoint at which the WebSocket implementation will make the endpoint available. The path may be a URI-string, which up to this point is the only kind of path we have used in any of the samples, but the path may also be a URI-template (level-1). URI-templates come in a variety of different levels of complexity, but the level-1–type templates are always of a form where one or more of the path segments of the URI is a variable and the variable is expressed in the shape {*varname*}, where *varname* is the name of the variable. Here are a few examples of valid paths:

```
/chat
/travel/hotels
/member/{level}
/cars/{make}/{model}
```

We will return to the topic of path mapping in the Java WebSocket API in Chapter 6.

The endpoint class property ties the class of the server endpoint to the configuration that it is using and ensures that the same `ServerEndpointConfig` instance is only used with one type of endpoint.

The subprotocols property defines a list of WebSocket subprotocol names that the server endpoint is willing to support, in order of preference, with its favorite subprotocol first. The extensions property defines a list of WebSocket extensions that the server endpoint is willing to use when its clients connect to it. This list is in order of preference, with the most preferred first in the list.

Shortly, we will talk about how a client and server endpoint decide on which subprotocol and which extensions they will use when the client attempts to initiate a connection.

The `ServerEndpointConfig.Configurator`, rather like the `ClientEndpointConfig.Configurator`, is a class that defines how the client side of the WebSocket opening handshake works. If you do not provide one, the WebSocket implementation will provide one for you. However, if you do provide a custom `ServerEndpointConfig.Configurator`, you are able to override some of the standard algorithms that are part of the opening handshake. Let's look at them:

```
public String getNegotiatedSubprotocol(List<String> supported,
                                        List<String> requested)
```

This method is called by the WebSocket implementation during the opening handshake when it needs to work out what WebSocket subprotocol is to be used for the connection. The supplied parameters are the lists of subprotocols supported by the server endpoint, and the list of subprotocols supplied by the client when it sent the opening handshake.

If you do not provide your own `ServerEndpointConfig.Configurator` that overrides this method, the WebSocket implementation will choose the first subprotocol in the list requested by the client that is supported by the server, or the empty string if there isn't one. For example, if the client requests

```
{'chat-53', 'chat', 'old-chat'}
```

and the endpoint has declared that it supports

```
{'chat-12', 'old-chat', 'chat', 'quick-chat'}
```

then the default implementation of this method will return the subprotocol `chat` because, even though the server endpoint supports `old-chat`, `chat` appears first in the requested list.

The next `ServerEndpointConfig.Configurator` method is

```
public List<Extension> getNegotiatedExtensions(
                        List<Extension> installed,
                        List<Extension> requested)
```

Like the `getNegotiatedSubprotocol()` method above, this method is called during the opening handshake to establish the WebSocket extensions that will be used should the connection be established. If the developer does not override this method, the WebSocket implementation will select, in the order requested, all the extensions the client asks for that are installed on the WebSocket implementation. The order returned can be very important. Imagine you had two WebSocket extensions that encoded outgoing WebSocket messages and decoded them for incoming WebSocket messages. Imagine that the first extension compressed the data and the second extension encrypted it. Clearly, it would be important to decode the extensions in the reverse order that they were encoded so that both ends would have to agree to apply the WebSocket extensions in the same order. The WebSocket implementation applies the extensions that are agreed on, according to this method, by applying them in the order they appear in the list returned from it. If you do intend to override this method, don't forget, as we saw for `ClientEndpointConfig.Configurator`, that you can query the WebSocket implementation for all the possible extensions installed on it by calling `WebSocketContainer.getInstalledExtensions()`.

The next method you can override by providing your own `ServerEndpointConfig.Configurator` class is this:

```
public boolean checkOrigin(String originHeaderValue)
```

All browser clients are supposed to include an HTTP Origin header along with their opening handshake request so that the WebSocket implementation can verify that it is initiating the WebSocket from a page that was loaded from the web server that the WebSocket implementation is part of. This method encapsulates that security check. Most developers will not need to override this, but it is there if a developer wants to provide a more stringent security check based on an unusual setup.

Whenever the WebSocket implementation needs to get an instance of a server endpoint because a new client has just connected, it calls the

```
public <T> T getEndpointInstance(Class<T> endpointClass)
                                     throws InstantiationException
```

method. The default WebSocket implementation of this method returns a new instance of the WebSocket endpoint each time it is called. This is how the WebSocket implementation is able to maintain precisely one instance

of a server endpoint per client connection. However, you may override
this method if you want some other kind of control over the number of
instances of the server endpoints. Some developers may design endpoints
in such a way that there is only one single instance of the server endpoint
that handles the connections from all possible clients. In this case, of course,
they will need to code the server endpoint defensively against multiple
concurrent incoming WebSocket lifecycle events: although the WebSocket
implementation will not allow more than one Java thread to call the server
endpoint at a time per client, if there are multiple clients, there may be
multiple threads. If you do wish to try this advanced mode of endpoint
configuration, then you would need to ensure that this method returns the
same, singleton instance of the server endpoint every time it is called.

Finally, the most powerful configuration method of the
`ServerEndpointConfig.Configurator` is the

```
public void modifyHandshake(ServerEndpointConfig sec,
                            HandshakeRequest request,
                            HandshakeResponse response)
```

method, which gives you complete read access to the opening handshake
request sent by the client when it attempts to connect. It also gives you
complete read/write access to the opening handshake response that
the WebSocket implementation creates immediately prior to sending
it back to the client. Those of you who have studied the exact formats
of the opening handshake request and responses will know that part
of the opening handshake response holds the subprotocol and extension
negotiation. These negotiations, as we saw earlier, are the result of calls
to other methods on the `ServerEndpointConfig.Configurator`. By
the time the `modifyHandshake()` method is called, the other methods,
`getNegotiatedSubprotocol()` and `getNegotiatedExtensions()`,
have already been called and the headers appropriately filled out on the
opening handshake response prior to passing it into the `modifyHandshake()`
method. Developers who override the `modifyHandshake()` method are
typically inserting some kind of implementation or application-specific HTTP
headers that further qualify the WebSocket connection that is being set up.
For example, perhaps the WhipImages'R'Us WebSocket application will
want to agree at the time of the opening handshake on the maximum size
of WebSocket message it is willing to accept. Such an implementation may
choose to define an HTTP header `WhipImagesRUs_Max-Message-Size`
that the client will send with a proposed maximum byte size of

WebSocket messages it is willing to handle, and the WhipImages'R'Us server implementation will respond by confirming the limit or by setting a lower limit on using the same header. In this case, the WhipImages'R'Us application would supply a custom `ClientEndpointConfig.Configurator` and a custom `ServerEndpointConfig.Configurator` to insert the `WhipImagesRUs_Max-Message-Size` headers with the appropriate values during the opening handshake.

As we leave our examination of the `ServerEndpointConfig` `.Configurator`, we note again that you can freely extend the `ServerEndpointConfig.Configurator` class with your own instance variables and methods.

**NOTE**
*Extending the `ServerEndpointConfig` `.Configurator` with your own data and methods is a really great way to make common information and behavior available to all the endpoint instances belonging to the same `ServerEndpointConfig`, whether you are using annotated or programmatic endpoints.*

# The WebSocket Session

If the `EndpointConfig` represents common state and algorithms common to all peers connecting to a WebSocket endpoint; the `Session` object represents all the common state associated with a single WebSocket connection from a peer to the endpoint. Client-side endpoints will only ever have a single `Session` object at a time, since client-side WebSocket endpoints only connect to a single server-side endpoint. Server-side endpoints will be associated with as many `Session` objects as there are client connections connecting to them. Either way, it is important to understand the possibilities for using the `Session` object, starting with its lifecycle.

## The Lifecycle of the WebSocket Session

The `Session` object is created upon the successful establishment of the WebSocket connection. It is assigned a unique identifier that may be accessed using the `getID()` call. The WebSocket implementation passes the newly created `Session` object into the open event handling method. In the case of an annotated endpoint, this is the method marked with the `@OnOpen` annotation; in the case of a programmatic endpoint, this is the `onOpen(Session session, EndpointConfig config)` call. At this point, the `session` is called open, and it is valid for use. We have already seen some of its functions in the Chat example and in earlier chapters. We summarize the functions here:

## Managing `MessageHandlers`

The `Session` object holds the configured `MessageHandlers` that are used to intercept WebSocket messages coming in on this connection. For annotated endpoint, the message handlers are implicitly defined by the method signature of the method or methods that are annotated by the `@OnMessage` annotation. For programmatic endpoints, the session's `MessageHandlers` are managed by the following three methods:

```
public void addMessageHandler(MessageHandler handler)
public Set<MessageHandler> getMessageHandlers()
public void removeMessageHandler(MessageHandler handler)
```

which allow the addition, listing, and removal of `MessageHandlers`, respectively. As we have seen, typically, programmatic endpoints add message handlers during the `onOpen()` call and do no further management of them on the `session`. Some WebSocket applications may, however, dynamically switch out `MessageHandler` classes at other points in the session's lifecycle, perhaps based on a particular client's changing needs.

## Obtaining the RemoteEndpoint

We have already seen that endpoints that need to send messages to their connected peer do so by obtaining a reference to the `RemoteEndpoint`, either the `RemoteEndpoint.Basic` or the `RemoteEndpoint.Async`, using the following methods:

```
public RemoteEndpoint.Basic getBasicRemote()
public RemoteEndpoint.Async getAsyncRemote()
```

We have already seen many uses of the `RemoteEndpoint.Basic` object. The `RemoteEndpoint.Async` object allows for the asynchronous sending of WebSocket messages, and we will be exploring its features in Chapter 5.

## Connection Properties

The `Session` object holds several properties that characterize the underlying connection. Some of them are not changeable once the `Session` has been established, an example being the subprotocol in use, which cannot be changed without restarting the connection because it is only negotiated between the client and the server during the opening handshake. Other properties such as the maximum idle timeout property, which governs the longest time the underlying connection may be idle before the WebSocket implementation is able to close it down due to inactivity, can be changed while the `Session` is open. Rather than step through all of the `Session` API for these properties, we will summarize them in the following table:

| Property | Use | Mutable? |
|---|---|---|
| maxBinaryMessageSize | The maximum size of an incoming binary message that will be handled | Yes |
| maxIdleTimeout | The longest a session can be inactive before it can be closed due to inactivity | Yes |
| maxTextMessageSize | The maximum size of an incoming text message that will be handled | Yes |
| negotiatedExtensions | The list of WebSocket extensions that were decided during the opening handshake | No |
| negotiatedSubprotocols | The WebSocket subprotocol that was decided during the opening handshake | No |
| protocolVersion | The version of the WebSocket network protocol in use | No |
| userPrincipal | The Java `UserPrincipal` representing the authenticated peer user | No |
| secure | Whether the underlying connection is encrypted | No |
| userProperties | A map applications may use to store information with the session | Yes |

## Path Properties

As we saw earlier in this chapter, server endpoints may be mapped either to a URI or to a URI-template (level-1). As we will see in Chapter 6 when we examine the path-mapping mechanisms in the Java WebSocket API in detail, when an opening handshake is made to a specific URI, if there is a match to a URI-template, the match will yield a list of path parameters where the variable segments correspond to specific values on the incoming URI. The incoming URI may also hold a query string with request parameters; all these aspects of the incoming URI are available from the `Session` object, as you can see in the following table:

| Method | Use |
|---|---|
| `URI getRequestURI()` | Returns the complete URI relative to the web application context root used by the connecting client |
| `Map<String,String>`<br>  `getPathParameters()` | Returns a map of the name-value pairs when the match with the request URI is to a URI-template |
| `String getQueryString()` | The query string of the request URI |
| `Map<String,List<String>>`<br>  `getRequestParameterMap()` | The request parameters extracted from the query string |

Here are some examples. If a server endpoint is mapped to

`/pets/cat`

and a client connects with the URI

`/pets/cat?color=black&fur=long`

then the request URI is `/pets/cat?color=black&fur=long`, the query string is `color=black&fur=long`, and the request parameters are (color, black) and (fur, long). The path parameters are empty because the endpoint is mapped to an exact URI.

If a server endpoint is mapped to

`/travel/{mode}/{level}`

and the incoming URI the client uses to connect is

`/travel/air/gold`

then the request URI is `/travel/air/gold`, the query string and request parameters are empty, and the path parameters are (mode, air) and (level, gold).

## Session Management

There are three methods that have to do with managing sessions. The isOpen() call allows you to determine if a session still represents an open connection. The getOpenSessions() allows you to list out all the open connections to the endpoint that the session you are calling it on is connected to, and the close() method allows you to close the connection.

The close() method comes in two flavors. The first with no parameters closes the connection with no particular descriptive information. The second allows you to pass in a reason, a CloseReason instance, for the closure. Since this information is transmitted to the peer when the connection is closed, it is a good idea to include a close reason.

**NOTE**
*A session being open is no guarantee that the underlying connection is active. It simply means that the WebSocket implementation has received no information to say that the connection has been closed. It may be that the connection has closed without telling anyone! If you really want to know if a Session represents an active connection, you should send a PingMessage on the connection and await a PongMessage to confirm the connection is working. In practice, on stable networks, a Session being open is usually a pretty good bet that you are able to send and receive messages through it.*

## Closing the Connection

When a connection is being closed, it may be happening for a number of reasons. The Session may be closed gracefully in response to the peer endpoint calling the close() method, in which case the local endpoint's close() handling method is called prior to the underlying connection actually being shut down. The Session may also be closed because the underlying connection has been found to have a problem and is already actually closed for business. In both cases, the close() handling method is called, but you need to use caution when using the Session object at this point in its life.

Care must be taken, however, in the implementation of the close()
handling method based on how the Session was closed. This means that you
cannot depend on being able to send any last messages from the close()
handling method. You can, however, depend on being able to retrieve any
stored application objects in the user property map on the Session object,
and note any of the other readable properties of the session, such as the
Session ID or the timeout interval.

Once the close() handling method has been called on the endpoint, the
session is closed, and you should not make any calls to it. In fact, most of
the methods of the Session will throw a runtime exception if you call them
after the Session instance has already closed.

**TIP**
*It is a good idea to use the close() handling
method to clean up any state you have stored in
the Session object before the Session object's
methods become inactive.*

# Summary

In this chapter, you have learned about two central objects in the Java
WebSocket API: the Session, which represents an active connection
between two WebSocket endpoints, and the EndpointConfig, which
holds information and methods that can be overriden and used to configure
a WebSocket endpoint. You saw by means of the Chat sample application
how the Session and EndpointConfig objects can be used to store
application state that is specific to a single peer and to all the peers of a
WebSocket endpoint, respectively.

# CHAPTER
## 5

## Advanced Messaging

I n this chapter, you will look at some of the more specialized forms of message processing in the Java WebSocket API. In Chapter 3, we examined the simpler synchronous forms of sending messages and some of the options for receiving messages. In this chapter, you will take a look at the asynchronous forms of message sending, the use of buffers for incoming messages, the configurable timeouts for send operations, and batching techniques. We will use the example of the MessageModes application to illustrate these advanced options for message processing.

# Checking Up on Your Connection: Pings and Pongs

We touched on the topic of ping and pong messages in Chapter 2. A *ping-pong interaction* is just the sending of a special kind of WebSocket message, called a *ping message*, and receiving in return another special (although almost identical) WebSocket message, called a *pong message*. You might wish to use a ping-pong interaction for a few reasons.

First, initiating a ping-pong interaction is a quick and dirty way of determining if the connection is actually working. Although you should be notified in your close event handlers if the connection is brought down, there are situations where this may not occur—for example, if the underlying socket has stopped responding because of a hardware failure.

Second, you might use them in order to keep a connection alive that otherwise might be closed due to a long period of inactivity. You will remember from Chapter 4 that you can configure the timeout property on the `Session` object if you want to, but you may not have control of the other end of the WebSocket connection—for example, if the peer of your connection is a non-Java implementation of the WebSocket protocol such as a browser. In such cases, sending a ping and waiting for a pong response acts as a manual way to prevent the timeout at both ends.

Third, you may wish to evaluate the health of the connection by timing how long a ping-pong interaction takes. This gives you a rough guide as to how much latency there might be in the connection. Ping and pong messages are only able to carry a very small payload of data, so a ping-pong interaction may not be a reliable guide as to how quickly large messages will flow backward and forward in an application, but it may provide some clues.

Both a ping and a pong message are able to carry a maximum of 125 bytes of binary data. In fact, a pong message that is the response to a ping message must carry the exact same binary data that was in the ping message.

In the Java WebSocket API, sending a ping message is done by the following method on `RemoteEndpoint`:

```
public void sendPing(ByteBuffer applicationData)
```

This method throws an `IOException` if there is a problem sending the message. You will recall from Chapter 2 that you listen for the returning pong message sent to you by your peer in response to the ping message in one of two ways. If you are writing an annotated endpoint, you would declare a message handling method that takes a `javax.websocket.PongMessage` as a parameter, such as the following code listing.

**Listing:**  *Example Pong Message Handler Method*

```
@OnMessage
public void catchPong(PongMessage pongMessage, Session session) {
     // ...
}
```

Alternatively, if you are creating a programmatic endpoint, you would create a message handler class that implements the `MessageHandler.Whole<PongMessage>` interface and configure it on the `Session` object representing the connection on which you sent the ping message.

You may be wondering at this point if there is anything special you have to do to your WebSocket application if you are on the receiving end of a ping message so that your application can respond properly if someone sends you one. The answer is that you do not have to do anything special: all Java WebSocket API implementations are required to respond as soon as they can to an incoming ping message with the appropriately formulated pong message. You do not have to write any code yourself that listens out for incoming ping messages and sends a pong message in reply.

The last use you may have for pong messages is that it is perfectly valid to send a pong message as a kind of unidirectional heartbeat: another means by which to keep a connection alive (or sniff out a dead one). In this case, you can send a pong message using the following method of the `RemoteEndpoint` interface:

```
public void sendPong(ByteBuffer applicationData)
```

The WebSocket peer at the other end of the connection is under no obligation to respond to an unsolicited pong message, so don't expect a reply if you send one.

If you do wish to listen out for unsolicited pong messages, then you do so in exactly the same way as you do for listening out for pong messages that are the response to a ping, as you saw previously.

# Sending WebSocket Messages Asynchronously

So far, in all our examples, we have only made use of the synchronous mode for sending messages. In other words, all the send methods that we have used have in some way blocked until the payload of the message was transmitted. This is a perfectly adequate way to send messages for many applications, particularly those that are sending only small messages. However, there are also many applications that wish to continue working in some way, even as the WebSocket messages are being sent. These tend to include applications that are sending very large messages, and that would rather be using processing power to formulate the next message. A photo processing application is a good example of this kind of application. Alternatively, there are many applications that initiate the sending of a message on a thread that may also be responsible for some other essential function of the application. Client-side GUI applications are a good example of this kind of application. WebSocket messages are sent from a thread that is also responsible for continuously updating the user interface in response to other inputs to the application. It may be quickly unacceptable to a user for the GUI to freeze while the application thread blocks until the transmission of a WebSocket message has completed.

Now we turn out attention to the `RemoteEndpoint.Async` interface. This interface provides an alternative view on the remote peer of a WebSocket connection, and a view that allows for a variety of ways to send a message without having to wait until it has been fully transmitted. You obtain a reference to the `RemoteEndpoint.Async` view of the peer of your WebSocket connection from the associated Session object using the following method call:

```
public RemoteEndpoint.Async getAsyncRemote()
```

The `RemoteEndpoint.Async` interface offers two ways in which to send a message asynchronously: *by future* or *with handler.*

# Sending a WebSocket Message by Future

The first way to send a WebSocket message asynchronously is referred to as "sending a WebSocket message by future." In this first mode, when you make the call to send, you obtain a reference to a `java.util.concurrent.Future` object. For example, the following is the method call to send a WebSocket text message by future:

```
public Future<Void> sendText(String text)
```

By the time the call returns and hands you this `Future` object, the message you passed in will probably not have been actually transmitted. The purpose of the `Future` object is to allow you to track the progress of the send operation you initiated by making method calls. This is a little like purchasing something online to be delivered to you: you are given a tracking number, which you can use to track the progress of the package as it makes its way to you. You can ask the `Future` object you obtain in this way if the message has been sent using the `Future.isDone()` call. You can cancel the send operation (assuming it has not already completed), using the `Future.cancel()` call. You can wait for the completion of the task using one of the `Future.get()` calls, which blocks until the message you passed in has been transmitted. If there is an error during transmission of the message, you will not know about it unless you explicitly query the `Future` object. This explains why the send methods that send a WebSocket message by future do not throw the exceptions that their synchronous counterparts on `RemoteEndpoint.Basic` do. You can find out if a message was transmitted properly by calling the `get()` method on the `Future` object. If there was no problem, this method returns with no return value. If there was a problem during transmission (perhaps a network failure, perhaps the message has taken too long to send), the method throws a `java.util.concurrent.ExecutionException`. The actual exception that was created to encapsulate the error raised during the faulty transmission can be obtained from the `ExecutionException` by calling the `ExecutionException.getCause()` method.

There are three API calls for sending WebSocket messages by future on the `RemoteEndpoint.Async` interface: one for sending text messages, one for sending binary messages, and one for sending custom developer objects.

**Listing:** *Methods for Sending a Message by Future*

```
public Future<Void> sendText(String text)
public Future<Void> sendBinary(ByteBuffer data)
public Future<Void> sendObject(Object data)
```

Each of the three API calls returns a `Future` object that follows the semantics that are described previously. If you have a custom object that you wish to send-by-future, you have to configure an appropriate `Encoder` for the object so that the WebSocket implementation is able to transform the custom object into a native WebSocket message prior to transmission, just in the same way as you would do for configuring the `Encoder` for a synchronous send operation. The `Encoder` is called prior to transmission in exactly the same way as it is for the synchronous call. The only difference is that the send API call returns prior to the encoding and transmission steps. If the encoder throws an exception while being asked to encode an object, the error is raised through the `Future` object—that is to say, is wrapped in the `ExecutionException` thrown by a call to one of the `Future`'s `get()` methods.

There is no special API for sending ping and pong messages by future, but don't worry. Because the payload of these messages is so small, it would barely make any difference if there was: the time between initiating the send and the actual transmission is likely to be very quick in most real settings.

## Sending a WebSocket Message with Handler

The second way to send a WebSocket message asynchronously is called "sending it *with handler*." When you send a WebSocket message using this mode, you are asked to supply a callback object. For example, if you wish to send a binary WebSocket message with handler, you would call the

```
public void sendBinary(ByteBuffer data, SendHandler handler)
```

method of `RemoteEndpoint.Async`, passing in the message data, and an instance of the `SendHandler` callback interface that you have implemented. The method returns immediately, and before the WebSocket message you supplied is transmitted. As the transmission of the message you passed in progresses, the WebSocket implementation will call your `SendHandler` implementation object to let you know how things went. The code listing that follows illustrates the `SendHandler` interface.

**Listing:** *The SendHandler Interface*

```
public interface SendHandler {
    public void onResult(SendResult result);
}
```

Because this is an interface with a single method, you have the choice as to whether to implement this as a regular Java class or as a Java SE 8 Lambda Expression. If the message is transmitted successfully, the WebSocket implementation will call your `SendHandler` implementation's `onResult()` method after the transmission has occurred with a `SendResult` object, which is in the OK state. You can determine this state by calling the `SendResult`'s `isOk()` method, which will yield `true` in this situation. If an error is raised during the transmission of the message, the WebSocket implementation calls your `SendHandler` implementation object's `onResult()` method with a `SendResult` that is not in the OK state. The exception can be retrieved for examination by calling the `SendResult`'s `getException()` method.

There are three API calls for sending WebSocket messages with handlers on the `RemoteEndpoint.Async` interface: one for sending text messages, one for sending binary messages, and one for sending custom object messages.

**Listing:** *Methods for Sending a Message with Handler*

```
public void sendText(String text, SendHandler handler)
public void sendBinary(ByteBuffer data, SendHandler handler)
public void sendObject(Object data, SendHandler handler)
```

Each of the three methods returns before transmission of the message. The `SendHandler` you pass in will be called with any problem in transmitting the message, if there is one. When using the `sendObject()` method, as with the `sendObject()` by future and the synchronous `sendObject()` calls, the WebSocket implementation will look for an appropriate Encoder with which to translate the custom object into a native WebSocket message. Any encoding errors that are raised during the translation phase prior to actually transmitting the message will also be reported to the `SendHandler` with a `SendResult` that holds the `EncodeException`. If all goes well, whichever message type you have and whichever method you choose, the `SendHandler` you pass in will be called with a `SendResult` set to the OK state.

As with send-by-future, there are no special methods for sending ping and pong messages with a callback handler.

# When to Send By Future and When to Send with Handler?

If you are designing an application that needs to send messages asynchronously, you are faced with a choice as to which mode to use: by future or by handler. Both modes give you exactly the same information about the status of the send: they inform you that a message has been transmitted, and they inform you if there was some kind of error that was generated during the transmission of the message. The send-by-future method allows you to intervene in the process by allowing you to cancel the transmission of the message, whereas the send with handler method does not give you that control.

To some extent, which mode you choose depends on a mix of your style of programming and how much you are willing to allow your application threads to be consumed with the task of monitoring whether a message has been sent or not. If you use the by future approach, then you will at some stage in the send process be devoting a thread either to checking in with the `Future` object to know if it has sent the message or not, or to blocking on the `get()` call until it has sent or throws an error indicating failure. You may have only a couple of things you need to do on the thread you use to initiate the send before you expect the confirmation to come back, in which case, calling the send-by-future method, taking care of those couple of things, and then calling the blocking `get()` call on the future object may be a perfectly fine approach. Alternatively, the thread you use to initiate the send may be responsible for some ongoing task that can never wait for any one part of the application to do lengthy processing, in which case you will not want that thread to wait on the `Future.get()` call. If you use the send-with-handler approach, the WebSocket implementation is responsible for using one of its own threads to notify you of the event (either success or failure) that concludes the attempt to transmit a message. For example, if you are sending messages from an application with a user interface, you may decide that you do not want to devote any of the user interface thread's time to awaiting a response because it has the continuous task of responding to asynchronous inputs of other kinds, like the user resizing the window. In this case, you would want the notification of the conclusion of the send process to happen on a different thread. That the WebSocket implementation will use one of its own threads to give you the SendHandler callback will be a very convenient option.

## Asynchronous Send Timeouts

One final level of control over the send process that you have when you use the RemoteEndpoint.Async asynchronous send calls is the ability to set a timeout. You could, of course, monitor the time it takes to send a message yourself, but it involves extra programming to monitor the amount of time that has passed and to attempt to abort the send operation. Much more convenient is to use the

```
public void setSendTimeout(long timeoutmillis)
```

method with a positive value to set an upper limit on the amount of time you are prepared to allow for the transmission of the message. The TimeoutException that is generated if the transmission of a message takes longer than the limit set using this method is passed into SendResult when the send-with-handler approach is used, and it is wrapped in the ExecutionException that is thrown by the Future's get() method when the by future method is used. If you do not want to wait indefinitely for messages to be sent either by future or sent with handler, you can set the value of this timeout to be any non-positive value.

# Message Batching

Some of the more sophisticated WebSocket implementations have a feature called *message batching*. This feature enables the WebSocket implementation to collect a number of outgoing messages on a connection until the size of the collection reaches some critical level. At that point, even though the application thinks it has sent the messages, the WebSocket implementation has not actually sent them on the connection. When the collection of messages, otherwise known as the *message batch*, reaches a critical size, the WebSocket implementation will actually transmit them. The WebSocket implementation will, of course, send the messages in the order that the application intended them to be sent. This approach can offer some big performance rewards, particularly for applications that send large numbers of messages in a short amount of time.

If a WebSocket implementation does support batching, WebSocket applications that wish to take advantage of the possible performance gains have to explicitly tell the implementation that they wish to allow it to use this technique. They do so by calling the following method:

```
RemoteEndpoint.setBatchingAllowed(boolean batchingAllowed)
```

Because the default value of this option is that batching may not be used for the messages sent on a `RemoteEndpoint`, if your application never calls this method to allow the batching technique to be applied, even on an implementation that supports it, none of the messages your application sends will be batched! This also means that if you do not care about message batching, whether or not the WebSocket implementation you use supports it, it will never be used on your application's messages as long as you never allow it for your applications.

However, once you allow a WebSocket implementation to batch your messages, you will need to remember that at any one point in time, you may have some unsent messages in a batch that has not yet been written to the WebSocket connection. This gives you an extra hurdle to clear when programming your application to take advantage of batching. In order to be sure that there are no unsent messages while using this batching mode, you can call the following, which sends any unsent messages:

```
RemoteEndpoint.flushBatch()
```

The kinds of performance improvements you might see when allowing a WebSocket implementation to use the message batching technique are likely to be highly dependent on a number of factors, including the following:

- The size of the messages your application sends
- The frequency with which it sends them
- The particular network on which you are sending the messages
- The performance characteristics of the peer WebSocket implementation receiving the messages you send

So in order to get the best results, you will likely need to do a lot of experimentation to determine if it is worth the extra step you need to take to allow this technique to be applied to your application.

If you run an application that uses the API to allow batching on a WebSocket implementation that does not support the batching technique, then the API calls will have no effect. The application will function correctly, but no messages will be batched.

If a WebSocket container does support message batching, the level at which it operates is below that of the asynchronous send API in the Java WebSocket API. To describe what this means more fully, consider an application that allows batching to run in a WebSocket implementation that does support the message batching feature. If the application uses an asynchronous send operation, it is considered complete in either of two circumstances:

- If the write to the batch will not cause the batch to be written to the underlying connection, then the operation is considered complete once the message has been written to the batch.

- If the write to the batch will cause the whole batch to be written to the underlying connection, then the operation is considered complete once the whole batch, including the latest message, has been written out.

This means that the callbacks to `SendHandlers`, and the return of the `Future.get()` methods, will occur in relation to the write to the batch, which may or may not be the same as the actual write of the message to the underlying connection.

# Buffering, Partial Messages, and Data Framing

You will remember from Chapter 2 that the WebSocket protocol may break up a WebSocket text or binary message into a sequence of smaller data frames that it actually sends on the WebSocket connection based on its own capacity or the network capabilities. There may or may not be a relationship between the data framing a WebSocket implementation uses and the representation of the message through the API. Specifically, if you elect to receive a message in pieces by means of declaring a method like the one shown in the following listing, the pieces you actually receive through this method may not be exactly the same as the pieces sent on the WebSocket connection by the WebSocket implementation.

**Listing:** *Example Method Handling a Message in Pieces*

```
@OnMessage
public void handleMessagePieces(String piece, boolean isLast) {
    // process each piece until the last piece arrives
}
```

For example, the WebSocket implementation may choose to buffer several incoming data frames into one piece. Equally, if you elect to receive WebSocket messages all in one piece, as you can see in this example:

```
@OnMessage
public void handleMessage(String wholeMessage) {
    //
}
```

and the peer of your connection sends you a WebSocket text message that arrives as a sequence of several data frames, each of which contains some smaller portion of the complete message, your WebSocket implementation has no choice but to buffer the pieces of the incoming message until the last piece arrives, and it can fit all the pieces of the jigsaw together and deliver the complete message using this method call.

In this way, WebSocket implementations support some form of buffering of incoming messages. In an application that deals with large messages, or an application that expects to have many clients sending messages, or an application that may encounter badly behaved clients that may occasionally attempt to send absurdly large messages, (or all three of those situations at once!), this kind of buffering may prove to be a problem. It may prove to be very expensive in terms of computing resources, or your application may not be designed to cope with such large messages. So you may want to be able to control the level of buffering you are willing to let the WebSocket implementation do for you.

In the Java WebSocket API, you have two controls by which to set limits on the level of buffering you wish the container to do in the circumstances described. The first programmatic approach allows you to directly control the buffer size limit for an individual connection, either for text or binary messages using the `Session` object's methods for binary and text messages respectively.

---

**Listing:**   *Session Methods for Controlling Incoming Message Buffers*

```
public void setMaxBinaryMessageBufferSize(int length)
public void setMaxTextMessageBufferSize(int length)
```

Once you have set the buffer size, any incoming messages that cause the buffer to overflow, such as a long sequence of incoming partial messages that exceed the capacity of the buffer used to reconstruct the message where the application has elected to receive it in complete form, will not be delivered. In such cases, the WebSocket endpoint's error handling method is called, and the connection is closed with the special-purpose `CloseReason.CloseCode.TOO _ BIG` code to describe the reason for the closure.

The other mechanism you can employ for annotated endpoints is to set a limit on the size of the message that can be delivered to a method annotated `@OnMessage`. Consider the example code listing that follows.

---

**Listing:**   *Example Message Handler with Limited Capacity*

```
@OnMessage(
      maxMessageSize= 64 * 1024
)
public void handleSmallMessages(byte[] data, Session session) {
      // messages are always 64kb or under.
}
```

This limits the size of the message that can be delivered to the method to 64KB.

**NOTE**
*Setting the buffer limits on the* `Session` *object gives you control over the buffer sizes used on a per-connection basis. You could have different buffer sizes for each connection in your application. The limit on the message size applies to messages being handled by the WebSocket endpoint with any client.*

# Guaranteeing Message Delivery

The WebSocket protocol offers no cast iron guarantee that WebSocket messages you send actually get properly received by the peer at the other end of the connection. In most cases, the WebSocket implementation will know if there is a problem during transmission of the message, but it can happen that the message does not get to the peer without any error being raised to you. So when considering the send operations of the Java WebSocket API, it is important to remember that the result of the send operation is telling you the message was transmitted, but not necessarily that it was received. If you do need to know for sure that WebSocket messages in your application are received by the intended recipients, you should consider programming some kind of return receipts that the recipient sends to confirm it actually got the message the sender sent. Fortunately, creating message handling methods that return a short acknowledgment of receipt is particularly easy using the @OnMessage annotation: simply include a return value on your method and it will be sent back immediately.

# Sending Messages API Summary

Finally, we conclude this section with a table that summarizes all the options for sending text, binary, ping, and pong messages using the RemoteEndpoint and its subclasses.

| Send Type and Payload | Mode | Interface | API |
|---|---|---|---|
| Pings and pongs | Sync | RemoteEndpoint | void sendPing(ByteBuffer b) |
| Text | Sync | RemoteEndpoint.Basic | void sendText(String text) |
| Text | Sync, sequence | RemoteEndpoint.Basic | void sendText(<br>    String textPart,<br>    boolean isLast) |
| Text | Async, future | RemoteEndpoint.Async | Future<Void> sendText(<br>    String text) |
| Text | Async, handler | RemoteEndpoint.Async | void sendText(String text,<br>    SendHandler handler) |
| Binary | Sync | RemoteEndpoint.Basic | void sendBinary(ByteBuffer b) |

| Send Type and Payload | Mode | Interface | API |
|---|---|---|---|
| Binary | Sync | `RemoteEndpoint.Basic` | `void sendBinary(`<br>`                ByteBuffer dataPast,`<br>`                    boolean isLast)` |
| Binary | Async, future | `RemoteEndpoint.Async` | `Future<Void>`<br>`    sendBinary(ByteBuffer b)` |
| Binary | Async, handler | `RemoteEndpoint.Async` | `void sendBinary(ByteBuffer b,`<br>`                SendHandler handler)` |
| Java object | Sync | `RemoteEndpoint.Basic` | `void sendObject(Object data)` |
| Java object | Async, future | `RemoteEndpoint.Async` | `Future<Void>`<br>`    sendObject(Object data)` |
| Java object | Async, handler | `RemoteEndpoint.Async` | `void sendObject(Object data,`<br>`                SendHandler handler)` |

# The MessageModes Application

Now that we have examined many of the more advanced topics of message processing in the Java WebSocket API, it's high time we rolled up our sleeves to look at some code. The MessageModes application is a client/server WebSocket application that exercises many of the advanced messaging features we have examined so far in this chapter.

## Overview of the MessageModes Application

The server side of the application is a simple, annotated server endpoint whose job it is to handle incoming text and binary messages, and report back to the client on what it receives.

The client side of the application is a Java Swing application that uses an annotated client endpoint to test all the send modes of the Java WebSocket API. You can send text or binary messages with a configurable size. The modes with which you can send the text and binary messages are

- Synchronous as a whole message

- Synchronous as a sequence of partial messages

- Asynchronous by future

- Asynchronously with handler

You can configure a timeout for the asynchronous send operations and see the response from the server endpoint when it receives a message. Finally, you can test the health of the connection by initiating a timed ping-pong interaction.

Figure 5-1 shows how the client application looks.

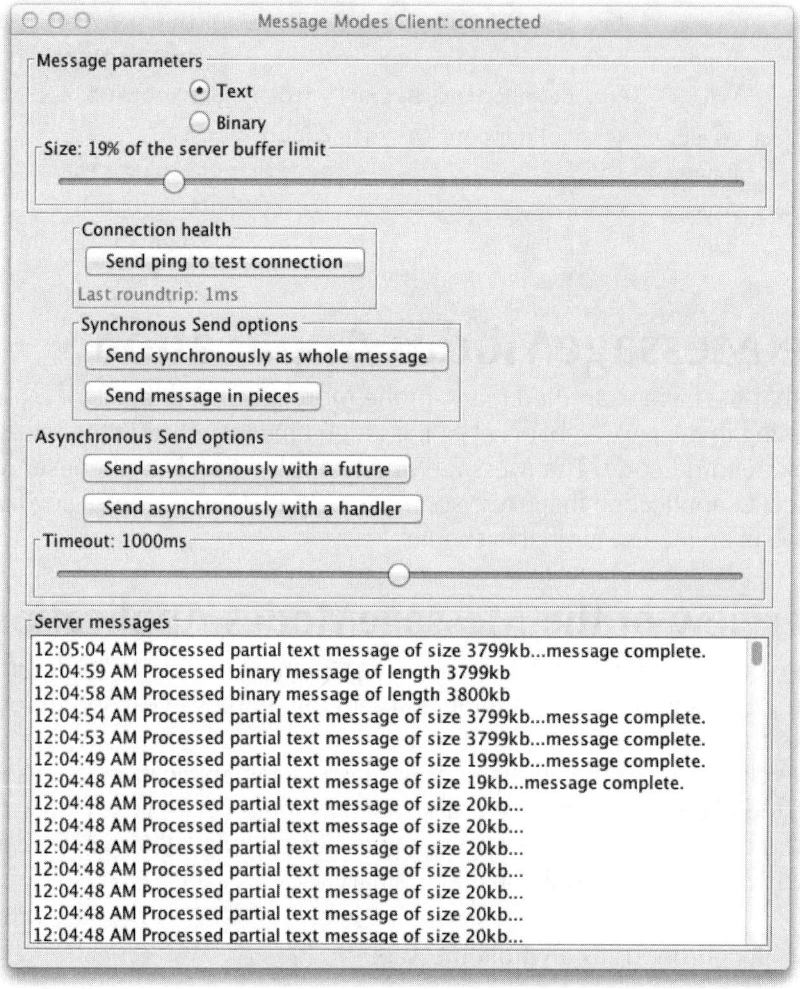

**FIGURE 5-1.** *The Message Modes window*

When choosing the message at the top of the screen, you can adjust the Size slider to formulate either a text or a binary message, depending on which you choose, ranging between approximately 300KB to almost 15MB. You will notice that when you move the slider all the way over to the right-hand side, the user interface informs you that the message you are about to send exceeds the maximum size limit on the server.

When you press the "send ping" button, the client application formulates a ping message and sends it. When the message returns, the client application notes the time it took to send and updates the user interface.

There are two buttons for sending the message you have created *synchronously*, one that sends the whole message all in one piece, and the second that sends the message as a sequence of 100 smaller pieces.

There are two buttons for sending the message you have created *asynchronously*, one that sends the message by future and the other that sends it with a handler. Below the buttons you can see a slider that you can use to configure an asynchronous send timeout anywhere between 0 seconds, indicating the send operation should never timeout, and 2 seconds.

Finally, the text area at the bottom of the window displays any server updates that are sent.

When you run the application, you should take some time to play with all the different options to get a general feel for all the different send modes in the Java WebSocket API. Be sure to try out different message sizes and asynchronous send timeouts and see what happens!

# Looking at the Code
# for the MessageModes Application

Let's continue the tour of this application by taking a look at some of the code that makes it work. First, let's take a look at the following code.

**Listing:** *The `MessageModesServer` Server Endpoint*

```
import java.io.IOException;
import java.text.DateFormat;
import java.util.Date;
import javax.websocket.*;
import javax.websocket.server.*;

@ServerEndpoint(value="/modes")
public class MessageModesServer {
    public static final int MESSAGE_MAX =  15 * 1000 * 1024;   // 15, 000 kb
```

```
@OnOpen
public void open(Session session) {
    session.setMaxBinaryMessageBufferSize(MESSAGE_MAX);
    this.reportMessage(session, "Connected !");
}

@OnMessage
public void binaryMessage(byte[] bytes, Session session) {
    this.reportMessage(session, "Processed binary message of length " +
                                bytes.length / 1024 + "kb");
}

@OnMessage(
    maxMessageSize = MESSAGE_MAX
)
public void textMessage(String partialMessage,
                        boolean isLast,
                        Session session) {
    String report = "Processed partial text message of size " +
                    partialMessage.length() / 1024 + "kb...";
    if (isLast) {
        report = report + "message complete.";
    }
    this.reportMessage(session, report);
}

public void reportMessage(Session s, String message) {
    try {
        String timeStamp =
            DateFormat.getTimeInstance().format(new Date());
        s.getBasicRemote().sendText(timeStamp + " " + message);
    } catch (IOException ioe) {
        System.out.println(ioe.getMessage());
    }
}

@OnError
public void error(Throwable t) {
    System.out.println("MessageModesServer error: " + t.getMessage());
}

@OnClose
public void close(Session s, CloseReason cr) {
    System.out.println("MessageModesServer closing because: " +
                       cr.getReasonPhrase());
}

}
```

The first thing the `MessageModesServer` endpoint does when a new connection is opened is to set a maximum limit on the size of the buffer the WebSocket implementation will use for buffering incoming binary messages. Then it reports a simple message back to the client that can be shown to the user of the application. You can see that it has two methods for handling incoming messages: one, its `binaryMessage()` method, which handles incoming binary messages, and which calls for the WebSocket implementation to deliver such messages in complete form as a byte array. The second handling method is `textMessage()`, which you will immediately notice is annotated in such a way as to limit the size of message that can be passed in to it using the `maxMessageSize` attribute of the `@OnMessage` annotation. This method elects to receive text messages in partial form. Both methods report back to the sender an informative message that confirms receipt of the incoming message in a user readable form.

Notice that the server endpoint uses the two different means to limit incoming message size. For binary messages, the limit is set on the binary data buffer used when the container needs to buffer incoming messages. For text messages, the limit is set on the size of the message that can be delivered to the message handling method. You will see in the material that follows that these different approaches have some subtly different outcomes at runtime.

Let's take a look now at the client endpoint, the `MessageModesClient` class. This is an annotated endpoint that manages all the WebSocket interactions between the Java Swing window (`MessageModesWindow`) and the server endpoint.

**Listing:**   *The MessageModesClient Client Endpoint*

```
import java.io.IOException;
import java.nio.ByteBuffer;
import java.util.concurrent.Future;
import javax.websocket.*;

@ClientEndpoint
public class MessageModesClient {
        private Session session;
        private MessageModesClientListener listener;
        static int PIECES_COUNT = 100;
        private int sendTimeout = 10;

        public MessageModesClient(MessageModesClientListener listener) {
            this.listener = listener;
        }

        public void setTimeout(int millis) {
            this.sendTimeout = millis;
        }

        @OnOpen
        public void open(Session session) {
```

```java
        this.session = session;
        this.listener.setConnected(true, null);
    }

    @OnMessage
    public void handleMessage(String message) {
        this.listener.reportMessage(message);
    }

    @OnMessage
    public void handlePong(PongMessage pm) {
        String sendAtString =
                    new String(pm.getApplicationData().array());
        long sendAtMillis = Long.parseLong(sendAtString);
        long roundtripMillis = System.currentTimeMillis() -
                                            sendAtMillis;
        this.listener.reportConnectionHealth(roundtripMillis);
    }

    @OnClose
    public void close(Session session, CloseReason cr) {
        this.listener.setConnected(false, cr);
    }

    public void disconnect() throws IOException {
        this.session.close(
            new CloseReason(CloseReason.CloseCodes.NORMAL_CLOSURE,
                                "User closed application"));
    }

    public void sendPing() throws IOException {
        long now = System.currentTimeMillis();
        byte[] data = ("" + now).getBytes();
        session.getBasicRemote().sendPing(ByteBuffer.wrap(data));
    }

    public Future<Void> sendAsyncByFuture(byte[] data)
                                        throws IOException {
        RemoteEndpoint.Async rea = session.getAsyncRemote();
        rea.setSendTimeout(this.sendTimeout);
        ByteBuffer bb = ByteBuffer.wrap(data);
        return rea.sendBinary(bb);
    }

    public Future<Void> sendAsyncByFuture(String textData)
                                        throws IOException {
        RemoteEndpoint.Async rea = session.getAsyncRemote();
        rea.setSendTimeout(this.sendTimeout);
        return rea.sendText(textData);
    }

    public void sendAsyncWithHandler(byte[] data, SendHandler sh) {
        RemoteEndpoint.Async rea = session.getAsyncRemote();
        ByteBuffer bb = ByteBuffer.wrap(data);
        rea.setSendTimeout(this.sendTimeout);
        rea.sendBinary(bb, sh);
    }
```

```java
public void sendAsyncWithHandler(String textData, SendHandler sh) {
    RemoteEndpoint.Async rea = session.getAsyncRemote();
    rea.setSendTimeout(this.sendTimeout);
    rea.sendText(textData, sh);
}

public void sendSynchronously(byte[] data) throws IOException {
    RemoteEndpoint.Basic reb = session.getBasicRemote();
    ByteBuffer bb = ByteBuffer.wrap(data);
    reb.sendBinary(bb);
}

public void sendSynchronously(String textData) throws IOException {
    RemoteEndpoint.Basic reb = session.getBasicRemote();
    reb.sendText(textData);
}

public void sendInPieces(byte[] data, PartialMessageSendListener pc)
                                                throws IOException {
    RemoteEndpoint.Basic reb = session.getBasicRemote();
    int chunkSize = (int) (data.length / PIECES_COUNT);
    BinaryDataIterator di = new BinaryDataIterator(data, chunkSize);
    int counter = 0;
    while (di.hasNext()) {
        ByteBuffer nextPiece = di.next();
        boolean isLast = !di.hasNext();
        reb.sendBinary(nextPiece, isLast);
        counter++;
        pc.reportProgress(counter);
    }
}

public void sendInPieces(String textData,
                         PartialMessageSendListener pc)
                                                throws IOException {
    RemoteEndpoint.Basic reb = session.getBasicRemote();
    byte[] bytes = textData.getBytes();
    int chunkSize = (int) (bytes.length / PIECES_COUNT);
    BinaryDataIterator di = new BinaryDataIterator(bytes,
                                                chunkSize);
    int counter = 0;
    while (di.hasNext()) {
        ByteBuffer nextPiece = di.next();
        boolean isLast = !di.hasNext();
        reb.sendText(new String(nextPiece.array()), isLast);
        counter++;
        pc.reportProgress(counter);

    }
}


}
```

We will not list the user interface code for this application, but take a look at the `MessageModesClientListener` interface. This interface embodies the updates the `MessageModesClient` endpoint needs to make to the user interface. In turn, the `MessageModesWindow` class, which holds all the GUI code for the client piece of the application, implements this interface, thereby allowing the `MessageModesClient` endpoint to keep the GUI up to date. Let's look at each of those updates, which are, of course, the individual methods on the `MessageModesClientListener` interface.

The method

```
public void setConnected(boolean isConnected, CloseReason cr)
```

is called by the client endpoint when its connection to the server is either opened or closed. When the connection is closed, it supplies the reason for the closure in the form of an instance of the `CloseReason` class. The method

```
public void reportMessage(String message);
```

is called by the client endpoint when it receives a message from the server endpoint. This is the call that the GUI uses to fill out the messages in the text area at the bottom of the window. The method

```
public void reportConnectionHealth(long millis);
```

is called by the client endpoint when it receives a pong in response to a ping with the time the roundtrip took, which in turn the GUI uses to update its display.

The `MessageModesClient` holds the local state of the session object to which it is connected. Notice that this is necessary because the `MessageModesClient` needs a reference to the session object outside the context of its lifecycle methods (which we already know can elect to have the session passed in to them). This is in contrast to the `MessageModesServer` endpoint, which only ever sends updates to the client in response to an incoming message. So in the server endpoint, it is not necessary to store the session as an instance variable. The other state is the timeout that is controlled by the slider widget in the user interface using the `setTimeout()` call.

The lifecycle methods of the `MessageModesClient` are relatively straightforward. The open handler method sets the session instance variable and notifies the GUI that the endpoint is connected. The close handler method informs the GUI that the endpoint has disconnected and why. The text message handler message notifies the GUI that the new message has arrived from the server. Let's just take a moment to look at the pong handling method.

You will notice from the `MessageModesClient` class's `sendPing()` method that the application data it sends inside the ping message is a byte array representation of the current time. You will remember that the obligation all Java WebSocket implementations have is to answer an incoming ping message as soon as it can with a pong message carrying exactly the same payload as was sent in the ping message. So you will see that the implementation of the pong handling method is relying on this requirement as it extracts the data from the pong message and interprets it as the time the ping message was sent in order to calculate the time the roundtrip took so that it can notify the GUI.

The rest of the methods on the `MessageModesClient` class are the eight send methods that the GUI calls for sending the messages. The operations include all four modes of sending a message, synchronously as a whole message, synchronously as a sequence of partial messages, asynchronously by future, and asynchronously with handler, for both text and binary messages.

# Things to Notice About the MessageModes Application

You'll notice that the two `MessageModesClient sendInPieces()` methods for sending a message synchronously as a sequence of partial messages, take a callback object, a `PartialMessageSendListener` instance that the method uses to report the progress of sending the pieces of the message. This is what powers the progress dialog you see when you send a message using this mode, shown in Figure 5-2, from the GUI, and which

**FIGURE 5-2.** *Sending a message in pieces*

illustrates one of the advantages of using this send mode: you can report progress every step of the way. You will also notice in the sendInPieces() methods that the MessageModesClient is responsible for deciding how granular to make the sequential send, another difference from the other modes.

The send-by-future methods, sendAsyncByFuture(), return the Future object to the GUI code, which results in the dialog in Figure 5-3, which pops up when you choose this mode to send the message and which allows the GUI to cancel the operation.

If you ask the GUI to send the message with a callback handler, assuming the message transmits successfully, you will see the dialog shown in Figure 5-4.

By examining the MessageModesClient's sendAsyncWithHandler() methods, you will see that the GUI code formulates the SendHandler implementation, which in turn causes this informational dialog to appear when the transmission is successful.

So far so good, but if you play with the MessageModes application a little more, you will notice that the messages are not always sent successfully. For example, if you turn up the message size to its maximum and choose to send a binary message synchronously in pieces, you should see the dialog shown in Figure 5-5.

This dialog appears because the method MessageModesServer is using to process the incoming sequence of binary messages is asking the WebSocket implementation to pass the message in as a complete byte array. In this situation, the WebSocket implementation running on the server side has no choice but to buffer the partial binary messages as they arrive. Yet the total size of these partial messages exceeds the maximum buffer size the MessageModesServer set on the session. So the WebSocket implementation on the server side closes the connection because the incoming message was

**FIGURE 5-3.**   *Sending a message by future*

**FIGURE 5-4.** *Sending a message with handler — transmission confirmed!*

too big and calls the error handling method of the server endpoint, notifying it of the error. The `MessageModesClient` receives the close notification, and in turn notifies the user interface, which pops up this dialog, giving the user the option to reconnect if she wants to.

You will also get this dialog if you attempt to send a text message that exceeds the limit set by the server endpoint.

Finally, if you adjust the asynchronous send timeouts to be small enough and attempt to send a message asynchronously, you will see the dialog shown in Figure 5-6.

This will happen, for example, when sending a message asynchronously with handler and with a low timeout. In this case, an asynchronous send operation yields a send result that the WebSocket implementation creates

**FIGURE 5-5.** *What happens when the message is too big*

**FIGURE 5-6.** *Timeout while sending a message*

when the operation times out. You can see this situation being modeled in the following excerpt from the `MessageModesWindow.sendCompleted()` method (being the send result, the client receives the `sendResult` variable in the excerpt when the operation times out).

**Listing:** *Excerpt from the MessageModesWindow Handling a SendResult*

```
if (sendResult.isOK()) {
    long millis = System.currentTimeMillis() - now;
    JOptionPane.showMessageDialog(this,
            "Message transmitted in " + millis + "ms" ,
            "Message Send Update",
            JOptionPane.INFORMATION_MESSAGE);
} else {
    String message = "Error sending message:\n" +
                    sendResult.getException().getMessage();
    Throwable ex = sendResult.getException();
    if (ex instanceof ExecutionException) {
        Throwable eex = ((ExecutionException) ex).getCause();
        if (eex instanceof java.util.concurrent.TimeoutException) {
            message = "Send timed out !\n
                            Try increasing the timeout...";
        }
    }
    JOptionPane.showMessageDialog(this,
                            message,
                            "Warning",
                            JOptionPane.ERROR_MESSAGE);
}
```

# Summary

This completes our look at the topic of advanced messaging. In this chapter, you have learned how to use the Java WebSocket API to send messages asynchronously, either using a `Future` object to track the progress of the transmission, or by supplying a `SendHandler` object that is called back when the transmission has concluded. You have learned how to configure timeouts for these send operations, and how to configure an application to limit the size of the incoming messages. You also learned that some WebSocket implementations include message batching features, and how to take advantage of those features when they are available.

# CHAPTER

## 6

# WebSocket Path Mapping

J ust as many of us are reachable by various addresses—e-mail, phone numbers, instant messaging handles, street addresses—server WebSocket endpoints have an address in the URI space of the server hosting them. You have already seen how client WebSocket endpoints connect to server endpoints, and you have seen how to map a server endpoint to a simple relative URI in the namespace of the web server. In this chapter, you will explore all the techniques for mapping server endpoints into the URI space of the web container hosting them, and how they can be best exploited in WebSocket applications. You will learn the nine rules of path mapping for the Java WebSocket API!

# Terminology of URIs

This book assumes you are familiar with URIs (uniform resource identifiers). However, the terminology around URI, URLs, and URNs can be used somewhat informally depending on the setting, so we start by defining a few terms that you will need to know in order to explore the capabilities of the path mapping mechanisms in the Java WebSocket API. The absolute URIs that refer to a WebSocket endpoint will all be of the form:

`<websocket-protocol-scheme>://<authority>:<port-number>/<uri-path>?<query-string>`

where

- The `websocket-protocol-scheme` is either `ws` or `wss` depending on whether the connection to the endpoint will not be encrypted or will be encrypted, respectively. We return to the topic of security in Chapter 7.

- The *authority* is usually just the hostname of the web server hosting the WebSocket endpoint.

- The *port number* is the number on which the web container hosting the WebSocket endpoint is listening for incoming opening handshake requests. For implementations of the Java WebSocket API, this is typically the same as the port number that the web server is listening to for HTTP requests of any kind, typically 8080.

- The *uri-path* is a string composed of path segments separated by the / delimiter. The path refers to some kind of resource—in our case, a possible WebSocket endpoint in the URI space of the web container.

■ The query string is a piece of data that qualifies the URI path. It takes the form of a list of request parameters, which are key value pairs: key=value separated either by & or by ;.

Here are some examples of WebSocket URIs:

■ ws://example.org/Play/tictactoe

■ wss://example.org:8000/FINANCE/secure/account-updates

■ ws://example.org:8080/websockets/Chat?mode=lazy&timeout=60

Request parameters are sometimes known as *query parameters*.

# WebSocket Path Mapping

There are two mechanisms for mapping server endpoints to paths in the Java WebSocket API: *exact URI mapping* and *URI template mapping*. We'll start with the mechanism you have already seen.

## Exact URI Mapping

As you have seen in all the examples so far in this book, you can map a server-side WebSocket endpoint to a URI path. A URI path is a non-absolute URI in this context that takes the form of the uri-path we defined previously and always begins with a /. Once you have decided on the path, you declare it in your WebSocket endpoint for annotated endpoints, as you can see in the listing that follows where the URI path is /tools/chat.

---

**Listing:** *Exact URI Mapped Annotated Endpoint*

```
@ServerEndpoint("/tools/chat")
public class MyChatServer {
    ...
}
```

Or, in the case of programmatic endpoints, when you create the `ServerApplicationConfig` implementation, you need to provide an instance of a `ServerEndpointConfig` for your endpoint, as you saw in Chapter 1. You supply the URI path when you create a

`ServerEndpointConfig` with the `ServerEndpointConfig.Builder`, as you can see in the listing that follows, where we are mapping this programmatic endpoint to the same path, `/tools/chat`.

**Listing:** *Configuring an Exact URI Mapped Programmatic Endpoint*

```
ServerEndpointConfig sec = ServerEndpointConfig.Builder
                  .create(MyChatEndpoint.class, "/tools/chat")
                  .build();
```

When you deploy either endpoint, you package the endpoint class (and additionally `ServerApplicationConfig` in the case of the programmatic endpoint) into a WAR file. When you create the WAR file, you are required to supply a URI path called the *context root of the web application*. The context root of a web application defines the root of the URI namespace for all the resources in the WAR file when it is deployed on the web server. So if, for example, the web server publishes its web applications to a namespace under a path /<web-apps>, like so:

```
<hostname> /<web-apps>
```

the root of the URI namespace for a WAR file can be accessed using the URI

```
<hostname>/<web-apps>/<context-root>
```

where `<context-root>` is the context root of the WAR file. Many web servers simply publish web applications to the root of their URI namespace (they use an empty path for the `<web-apps>` path).

Here is the first rule of URI mapping for the Java WebSocket API.

### Rule 1: The URI path of a server WebSocket endpoint is treated by web servers as relative to the web application context root of the web application in which it is deployed.

Therefore, the absolute WebSocket URIs used to access server endpoints mapped to a URI path will look like this, with possibly a query string at the end, as you shall see:

```
<ws or wss>://<hostname<:<port>/<webserver-root>/<context-path>/
                                  <websocket-uri-path>
```

So, for example, if you packaged either endpoint into a WAR file with context-root equal to /employee and deployed it to a web server that publishes web applications to the root of its namespace, you would be able to access the endpoint by connecting to

```
ws://example.org/employee/tools/chat
```

Rule 1 should already be very familiar to you: all the server endpoints so far in this book have used exact URI mappings. They have been accessed from their respective clients with absolute URLs that are derived by applying Rule 1 to the URI path of the server endpoint.

Now, if you tried to deploy both the annotated endpoint and the programmatic endpoint listed in the preceding example snippets as part of the same web application, you would find that the Web Socket implementation would reject the WAR file because of Rule 2.

### Rule 2: No two endpoints with the same URI path may be deployed in the same web application.

The reason for this rule is, we hope, already obvious to you: if you were allowed to deploy both the annotated and the programmatic endpoint, then they would both be published under the same absolute URI by the web server:

```
ws://example.org/employee/tools/chat
```

So when a client tried to connect to this URI, the web server would have no indication as to which endpoint to deliver the opening handshake to. If you try to deploy an application that breaks this rule, the WebSocket implementation will fail the deployment.

You could, of course, deploy both endpoints to the web server without changing the URI paths you mapped each WebSocket to, but you would have to put each endpoint into a different web application. By doing so, you would be required to provide two distinct context roots and the web server would no longer be confronted with attempting to publish two web resources to the same URI in its own namespace.

Let's consider Rule 3.

### Rule 3: URI paths are treated by web servers case sensitively.

This means that within the same web application, with context root /garden, you could deploy two endpoints such as these:

```
@ServerEndpoint("/orchard")
public class MyAppleTrees {
    ...
}
```

and

```
@ServerEndpoint("/Orchard")
public class MyPearTrees {
    ...
}
```

A request to

```
ws://example.org/garden/Orchard
```

would connect you to the pear trees, while a request to

```
ws://example.org/garden/orchard
```

would connect you to the apple trees.

# URI Template Paths

The second kind of path you can use to publish a server endpoint is called a URI template. A URI template is defined as a compact sequence of characters for describing a range of URIs through variable expansion. In other words, a URI template is like a URI, except that parts of the URI have been replaced by variables. Before you look more into URI templates, here is a simple example of a relative URI template:

```
/travel/{access-level}/flights
```

In this URI-template, one of the path segments has a representation as a variable, access-level. URI templates are useful because, by representing segments of the URI as variables, a URI template can actually represent a range of URIs, each of which is the same as the URI template if the URI template assumes fixed values for each of the variable pieces. For example, the URI template is equivalent to the following URIs:

`/travel/business/flights`, when the access-level variable is vip
`/travel/coach/flights`, when the access-level variable is coach.

A URI that is equivalent to a URI template with specific values set for the variables is described as a *valid expansion* of the URI template.

The following is an example of a WebSocket server endpoint mapped to the example URI template:

```
@ServerEndpoint("/travel/{access-level}/flights")
public class BookingService {
    . . .
}
```

You can easily imagine the code that would create a `ServerEndpointConfig` with the same path, `/travel/{access-level}/flights`, which could be used to configure a programmatic endpoint.

Now we come to Rule 4.

> **Rule 4: An incoming opening handshake matches a server endpoint mapped to a URI template path if the request URI of the opening handshake is a valid expansion of the URI template.**

Using Rule 4, you can see that if our `BookingService` endpoint is deployed at fun.org within a WAR file with context root `/customer/services`, a client could connect to the `BookingService` with any of the following URIs:

```
ws://fun.org/customer/services/travel/vip/flights
ws://fun.org/customer/services/travel/premier/flights
ws://fun.org/customer/services/travel/executive/flights
ws://fun.org/customer/services/travel/cattleclass/flights
```

The value of the access-level variable would be `vip`, `premier`, `executive`, and `cattleclass`, respectively.

There are several different levels of complexity of URI templates out in the wild. You have just seen an example of simple variable substitution. There are more complex levels that include regular expressions on portions of the URI, whose expansions are calculated using regular expression matching. The Java WebSocket API allows only the simpler forms of URI templates, which brings us to Rule 5.

> **Rule 5: For mapping server endpoints, the Java WebSocket API allows URI templates level 1 only.**

Level-1 URI templates allow only path variables that are single named variables that are enclosed in {} and do not contain any URI reserved characters such as +, *, or /. This means that the following URI templates are level 1, and are therefore allowable as WebSocket endpoint paths:

```
/{foo}
/street/{number}/{directionality}
/{color}/trees/{seasonality}/{name}
```

but the following expressions are not

```
/{*}/foo
/{+day}/pants
/map/{x,y}
/{keys*}
/location/{country/county}
```

This brings a simplicity to the matching scheme for the Java WebSocket API at the cost of ultimate flexibility. Nevertheless, from now on we will use the term URI template as a shorthand for URI templates level 1 only because they are the only ones allowed in the Java WebSocket API. The matching rule for URI templates is covered by Rule 6.

**Rule 6: An incoming URI is a match of a URI template level 1 path if, and only if, each variable in the URI template can be expanded with a non-empty value such that the resulting expansion is exactly the same as the URI.**

## APIs Relating to URI Template Matching

The usefulness of using URI templates to map a server endpoint is not limited to allowing multiple URIs to connect to a published endpoint, but to make use of the values of the URI template variables that are a byproduct of the match. For example, to continue with the previous BookingService example, if we are able to connect to our BookingService endpoint using the following URI:

```
ws://fun.org/customer/services/travel/vip/flights
```

we might expect a better level of service and options (and price!) than if we connected to the BookingService endpoint using this URI:

```
ws://fun.org/customer/services/travel/cattleclass/flights
```

In order to stratify the levels of service, the `BookingService` endpoint needs to be able to access the values of the variables produced by the match on the incoming URI.

The JavaWebSocket API offers two ways to do this. First, and available to both annotated endpoints and programmatic endpoints, the `Session` object holds these variables available by calling

```
public Map<String, String> getPathParameters()
```

which returns a map where the keys are the path parameter variable names—that is to say, the { } enclosed strings in the URI template—and the map values are the values the variables take in matching incoming URIs.

**Listing:**   *An Annotated Endpoint Using a URI Template*

```
@ServerEndpoint("/travel/{access-level}/flights")
public class BookingService {

    @OnOpen
    public void processNewClient(Session session) {
        Map<String, String> pathParameters =
                            session.getPathParameters();
        String memberLevel = pathParameters.get("access-level");
        switch (memberLevel) {
            case "vip":
                this.offerBestSeatsAndPriorityDeals();
            default:
                this.offerCheapSeats();
        }

    }
...
}
```

If you are developing annotated endpoints, you have a second option for accessing the path parameters on the incoming URI, by using the `@PathParam` annotation. The `@PathParam` annotation has a single value attribute, which is the name of the path parameter you are looking for the value of. For any of the lifecycle methods (those annotated with `@OnOpen`, `@OnMessage`, `@OnError`, `@OnClose`), by including a `String` valued method parameter marked with the `@PathParam` annotation that carries the name of a variable in the URI template, the WebSocket implementation will pass the value of the parameter to be the value of the path parameter to the method. In this way, you can include multiple `String` valued method parameters marked with the `@PathParam` annotation, provided each `@PathParam` annotation name corresponds to a variable name in the URI template.

For example, you could rewrite the `BookingService` endpoint as it appears in the listing that follows.

**Listing:** *An Annotated Endpoint Using a URI Template Accessing a Path Parameter*

```
@ServerEndpoint("/travel/{access-level}/flights")
public class BookingService {

    @OnOpen
    public void processNewClient(
                @PathParam("access-level") String memberLevel) {
        switch (memberLevel) {
            case "vip":
                this.offerBestSeatsAndPriorityDeals();
            default:
                this.offerCheapSeats();
        }

    }

    public void offerBestSeatsAndPriorityDeals() {}
    public void offerCheapSeats() {}

}
```

In this example, we are asking for the access-level variable by annotating the `String memberLevel` method parameter with the `@PathParam("access-level")`. If we had more variables in the URI template that we used to publish the endpoint, we could retrieve them at runtime from any of the lifecycle methods simply by using multiple method parameters, each parameter annotated with a suitable `@PathParam` annotation.

There are a number of options for the type of method parameters used with `@PathParam`. The most obvious and probably most commonly used type is `String`, as you saw in the example, but you are also allowed to have a Java primitive type, or class equivalent thereof. This makes things a little more convenient and cleaner in your code if you are thinking of the values of a path parameters as numbers, for example. In these cases, the WebSocket implementation will attempt to decode the value of the path parameter produced by the match with the incoming URI into the type requested. It will do this by looking for the single string argument constructor on the Java primitive class and using it to construct the instance. The following example uses the path parameter to indicate which level of the hotel star classification scheme to use in an advertising banner powered by WebSockets.

**Listing:** *Accessing a Path Parameter as an int Value*

```
@ServerEndpoint("/travel/hotels/{stars}")
public class HotelBookingService {

        @OnMessage
        public void startAdvertisingBanner(String resortCode,
                                    @PathParam("stars") int hotelStars) {
            switch (hotelStars) {
                case 5:
                    this.broadcastDeluxeProperties();
                case 4:
                    ...
            }

        }
    }
}
```

In this example, if a client connects to the service using the following URI:

```
ws://fun.org/customer/services/travel/hotels/4
```

then the WebSocket implementation will parse out the "stars" path parameter, which has a value of 4. Then it will pass in the int value hotelStars to the startAdvertisingBanner() method with the value 4 that it obtained by calling code equivalent to the following:

```
int hotelStars = (new Integer("4")).intValue();
```

Of course, it may not be possible for the WebSocket implementation to convert the URI the client used to connect to the WebSocket into the type requested in one of the lifecycle methods on the annotated endpoint. If the endpoint sticks to asking for path parameters in the form of the String type, then this is never a problem because no conversion is needed. But as soon as you elect to receive the path parameters as a different Java type, the conversion may not be possible. In our example, a client could perfectly well connect to the HotelBookingService endpoint using the following URI and then send it a message:

```
ws://fun.org/customer/services/travel/hotels/oops
```

At this point, the path parameter value is the string `oops`, but the message handling method looks like this:

```
@OnMessage
public void startAdvertisingBanner(String resortCode,
                        @PathParam("stars") int hotelStars)
```

The WebSocket implementation is being asked to convert the string `oops` into an int, which of course it cannot do. In this case, and all such conversion failure cases, the WebSocket implementation will not be able to call the message handler method and will instead generate an error (a `DecodeException`), which it passes to the error handling method declared on the endpoint, or logs it for future examination if none has been defined. This type of conversion error doesn't cause the connection to close, but of course, if you decide to, you could close the connection in the error handling method with an informative `CloseReason`, which the client would be able to look at.

Before we move from the topic of URI templates in the Java WebSocket API, we come to the next rule, which deals with what happens when a WebSocket application contains two URI templates that are *equivalent*. Two URI templates are said to be *equivalent* in the Java WebSocket API if they have path variables at the same positions in the uri-path, and the same values in the path segments that are not variables. Note that two URI templates with path variables at the same positions in their uri-paths can be equivalent even if they use different variable names in the variable segments. So, for example, the following two URI templates are considered equivalent in the Java WebSocket API:

```
/{member-level}
/{access-code}
```

Also considered equivalent are

```
/booking/{transport-mode}/europe
/booking/{name}/europe
```

and

```
/a/{b}/c/{d}
/a/{x}/c/{y}
```

Now let's look at Rule 7, which gives an analogous rule for equivalent URI templates as Rule 2 does for equal URI paths:

**Rule 7: No two endpoints with the equivalent URI templates may be deployed in the same web application.**

The reason for this rule is not hard to guess: if the Java WebSocket API allowed multiple endpoints mapped to equivalent URI templates in the same web application and a client tried to connect to the web application with a URI that was a valid expansion of the URI template, it would not be possible to work out which endpoint the client should be connected to!

As with Rule 2, if you try to deploy an application that breaks this rule, the WebSocket implementation will fail the deployment.

# Accessing Path Information at Runtime

Now that we have covered the two mechanisms for publishing endpoints into the URI space of the WebSocket implementation, let's pause here before we look at some additional options that build on these mechanisms to look at some of the APIs that relate to the paths in use in a running WebSocket server application.

First, you can always obtain the path under which the WebSocket implementation has published the endpoint from the endpoint's `ServerEndpointConfig` object by calling the

`public String getPath()` method. This technique works equally well whether the endpoint is mapped to an exact URI or to a URI template. Here is an example:

**Listing:**  *An Endpoint Accessing Its Own Path Mapping*

```
@ServerEndpoint("/travel/hotels/{stars}")
public class HotelBookingService {

        public void handleConnection(Session s, EndpointConfig config) {
            String myPath = ((ServerEndpointConfig) config).getPath();
            // myPath is "/travel/hotels/{stars}"
      ...
}
```

The second piece of information you may wish to access at runtime from within an endpoint is the URI that the client used to connect to it. This information is available in a variety of forms as you shall see later, but the workhorse method that contains all the information is

```
Session.getRequestURI()
```

This gives you the URI path relative to the web server root of the WebSocket implementation. Notice that this includes the context root of the web application that contains the WebSocket. So, for example, in the hotel booking example, suppose the `HotelBookingService` endpoint is deployed in a web application with context root `/customer/services`. Now suppose a client has connected to the endpoint with the URI

```
ws://fun.org/customer/services/travel/hotels/3
```

then the request URI that the `HotelBookingService` endpoint will get from the `Session` by calling `getRequestURI()` is

```
/customer/services/travel/hotels/3
```

There are two more methods on the `Session` object that parse further information from this request URI when the request URI includes a query string. So let's take a look at query strings.

## Query Strings and Request Parameters

As you saw at the beginning of the chapter, following the URI path of a WebSocket endpoint is the optional query string

```
<websocket-protocol-scheme>://<authority>:<port-number>/<uri-path>?<query-string>
```

Query strings in URIs originally became popular in CGI (Common Gateway Interface) applications. The uri-path portion of a URI would locate the CGI program (often `/cgi-bin`) and the query string appended after the uri-path would supply a list of parameters to the CGI program to qualify the request. The query string is also commonly used when posting data using an HTML form. For example, in a web application, in the following HTML code

```
<form name="input" action="form-processor" method="post">
        Your Username: <input type="text" name="user">
                        <input type="submit" value="Submit">
    </form>
```

pushing the submit button produces an HTTP request to the URI

```
/form-processor?user=Jared
```

relative to the page holding the HTML code, and where the input field contains the text `Jared`. Depending on the nature of the web resource located at the uri-path `/form-processor`, the query string `user=Jared` can be used to determine what kind of response should be made. For example, if the resource at form-processor is a Java Servlet, the Java Servlet can retrieve the query string from the `HttpServletRequest` using the `getQueryString()` API call.

In a similar spirit, query strings can be used in the URIs used to connect to WebSocket endpoints created using the Java WebSocket API. This brings us immediately to Rule 8.

### Rule 8: A query string sent as part of the request URI of an opening handshake request is not used by the Java WebSocket API to determine the endpoint to which it may match.

In other words, whether or not a request URI contains a query string or not makes no difference to whether it will match a server endpoint's published path. Additionally, query strings are ignored in paths used to publish endpoints.

Just as CGI programs did and other kinds of web components do, WebSocket endpoints can use the query string to further configure a connection a client is making. Because the WebSocket implementation essentially ignores the value of the query string on an incoming request, any logic that uses the value of the query string is purely inside the WebSocket component. The main methods you can use to retrieve the value of the query string are all on the `Session` object

```
public String getQueryString()
```

which returns the whole query string (everything after the ? character) and

```
public Map<String,List<String>> getRequestParameterMap()
```

which gives you a data structure with all the request parameters parsed from the query string. You'll notice that the values of the map are lists of strings; this is because a query string may have two parameters of the same name, but different values. For example, you might connect to our `HotelBookingService` endpoint using the URI

```
ws://fun.org/customer/services/
            travel/hotels/4?showpics=thumbnails&description=short
```

In this case, the query string is `showpics=thumbnails&description=short`, and to obtain the request parameters from the endpoint, you might do something like what you see in the following code listing, where the values of `pictureType` and `textMode` would be `thumbnails` and `short`, respectively.

**Listing:** *Accessing Request Parameters*

```
@ServerEndpoint("/travel/hotels/{stars}")
public class HotelBookingService {
    @OnOpen
    public void handleConnection(Session session,
                                        EndpointConfig config) {
        String pictureType =
            session.getRequestParameterMap().get("showpics").get(0);
        String textMode =
            session.getRequestParameterMap().get("description").get(0);
        ...
    }

    @OnMessage
    public void startAdvertisingBanner(String resortCode,
                            @PathParam("stars") int hotelStars) {
        switch (hotelStars) {
            case 5:
                this.broadcastDeluxeProperties();
            case 4:
                ...
        }

    }

}
```

**NOTE**
*You can also get the query string from the request URI. In the Java WebSocket API, the `Session.getRequestURI()` call always includes both the uri-path and the query string.*

Now that you have explored the mechanisms of URI templates and their path parameters, and query strings and their request parameters, you may be wondering when to use which mechanism, if at all. We will return to this topic toward the end of the chapter.

# Matching Precedence

Many, if not most, WebSocket applications will contain more than one endpoint. Thanks to Rule 2, you know that in WebSocket applications that use only exact URI paths to publish WebSocket endpoints, each WebSocket endpoint path must have a different value. But in a WebSocket application that also contains endpoints mapped to URI templates, it is possible to have a situation where two endpoint paths could possibly both match an incoming request URI. For example, suppose you have a WebSocket application containing endpoints `ClementineEndpoint` and `CitrusEndpoint`. These endpoints are mapped as follows:

`ClementineEndpoint` is mapped to `/clementine`
`CitrusEndpoint` is mapped to `/{fruit}`

It is clear by the rules we already have that a client request for

`ws://fruits.org/fruit-app/lemon`

or

`ws://fruits.org/fruit-app/grapefruit`

will both connect to the `CitrusEndpoint`. But what about the following URI:

`ws://fruits.org/fruit-app/clementine`

The answer is that the client using this URI will connect to the ClementineEndpoint endpoint because the JavaWebSocket API prefers exact matches. Because the paths used to publish server endpoints may have multiple segments, the Java WebSocket API compares the incoming URI with each endpoint path, reading each path segment of the URI path from left to right, preferring at each segment an exact match over a match with a variable segment. This gives you Rule 9.

**Rule 9: When determining which of several URI path and URI template paths in a WebSocket application match an incoming URI, the Java WebSocket API compares path segment by path segment, starting from the left, preferring at each segment an exact match over a match with a path variable.**

Before we move on to looking at an application that uses some of the path mapping features we have been looking at, let's look at some examples of these mapping precedence rules in action.

Let's look at an application that has three endpoints:

endpoint `Apple`, mapped to `/fruit/{plant-type}/thin`

endpoint `Blackberry`, mapped to `/fruit/bush/thin`

endpoint `Clementine`, mapped to `/fruit/{plant-type}/{skin-type}`

Note that these URI template paths can all coexist in the same WebSocket application because no two are equivalent to each other. Now, if your client connects to the following URI, it won't match any of the endpoints because the match is case sensitive (see Rule 3):

`ws://fruits.org/sweet-ones/fruit/bush/Thin`

If your client connects to the URI

`ws://fruits.org/sweet-ones/fruit/bush/thin`

there will be a match with the `Blackberry` endpoint, but not the `Apple` or `Clementine` endpoints, because an exact match is preferred over a match to a URI template. If your client connects to the URI

`ws://fruits.org/sweet-ones/fruit/tree/thin`

it will get a match with the `Apple` endpoint with variable plant-type equal to `tree` because an exact matching segment is preferred over a variable segment (Rule 9), which rules out the `Clementine` endpoint, which could possibly have matched.

Finally, if your client connects with the incoming URI

`ws://fruits.org/sweet-ones/fruit/evergreentree/thick`

it will get a match with the `Clementine` endpoint, the plant-type path parameter value `evergreen`, and the `skin-type` path parameter value `thick` because the incoming URI is a valid expansion of the URI template to which it is mapped, and because it doesn't match either of the other two.

Finally, as an illustration of the rather lengthy Rule 9, suppose you have two travel endpoints in a web application with the context path transport:

endpoint `Plane` mapped to the URI-template: `/{speed}/luxurious`

endpoint `CruiseLiner` mapped to the URI-template: `/slow/{comfort}`

If the client connects to the application with the incoming URI:

```
ws://fun.org/transport/slow/luxurious
```

the URI matches the `CruiseLiner` with the comfort path parameter value `luxurious`, not the `Plane` with the speed path parameter value `slow`. This is because the Java WebSocket API's matching precedence of exact matches over variable matches works from left to right.

# The Portfolio Application

In order to give you some ideas as to when you to use exact URI path mapping and when to use URI templates, let's turn to the Portfolio application. The Portfolio application is a client server WebSocket application. The client is a simple JavaScript client; the server is a single WebSocket endpoint created using the Java WebSocket API. When the client page opens, the JavaScript client connects to the server endpoint, which in turn broadcasts a sequence of updates on a portfolio of stocks back to the client. The goal of this application is to easily be able to embed data that is being frequently updated to some portion of a larger web page. Depending on what URI the client uses to connect to the server endpoint, the updates will contain more or less detailed information on the changing prices and volumes of the stock data in the portfolio, and will be delivered in more or less timely and attractive fashions.

Let's take a look at the Portfolio application in action.

At the top of the page is a control panel that allows you to formulate which of the stock data fields you want to see in your updates, and allows you to choose which level of access you want to have. Below the control panel is the output area, which updates each time the server endpoint sends out an update on the portfolio according to the parameters you requested.

You'll notice that at the bronze level (Figure 6-1), your stock quotes are delayed 20 minutes. As you move up to the silver level, you get a new color scheme and the quotes are more recent and occur more frequently. At the gold level, the quotes are tracking the market without delay, and you have a more attractive color scheme to reflect your elevated status. Figure 6-2 illustrates the gold access level, with all the data fields showing.

Each time you change an option in the control panel, the JavaScript client is closing the existing connection and reestablishing a new connection. All the information about the member level and the data fields you wish to see

**FIGURE 6-1.** *The portfolio application at Bronze level*

is carried in the URI the JavaScript uses to connect each time, and in fact the client never sends the server a WebSocket message at all; the client only listens in for update messages from the server. When the client receives an update message from the server endpoint, it displays the content on the web page.

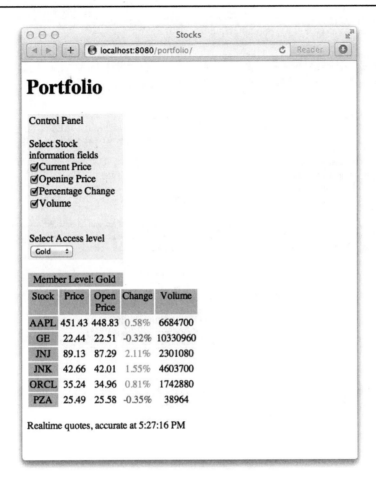

**FIGURE 6-2.** *The Portfolio application at the Gold level*

Let's take a look at the most important part of this application, the
`PortfolioBroadcastEndpoint`.

**Listing:** *The Portfolio Endpoint*

```
import java.io.*;
import java.util.*;
import javax.websocket.*;
import javax.websocket.server.*;
```

```java
@ServerEndpoint(
        value="/updates/{access-level}",
        encoders={PortfolioUpdateEncoder.class}
)
public class PortfolioBroadcastEndpoint implements StockDataSourceListener {
        private Session session;
        private StockDataSource dataSource;

        @OnOpen
        public void startUpdates(Session session,
                    @PathParam("access-level") String accessLevel)
                                                throws IOException   {
            this.session = session;
            MemberLevel memberLevel;
            memberLevel = MemberLevel.create(accessLevel);
            Map<String, List<String>> requestParams =
                        session.getRequestParameterMap();
            DataOptions options =
                        this.parseOptionsFromRequestParams(requestParams);
            this.dataSource = new StockDataSource(options, memberLevel);
            this.dataSource.addStockDataSourceListener(this);
            this.dataSource.start();
        }

        public void handleNewStockData(PortfolioUpdate pu)  {
            try {
                session.getBasicRemote().sendObject(pu);
            } catch (IOException | EncodeException ioe) {
                this.processError(ioe);
            }
        }

        @OnError
        public void processError(Throwable t) {
            System.out.println("Error: " + t.getMessage());
        }

        @OnClose
        public void stopUpdates(Session session) {
            dataSource.stop();
        }

        public DataOptions parseOptionsFromRequestParams(Map<String,
                                        List<String>> requestParams) {
            DataOptions options = (new DataOptions())
        .currentPrice(requestParams.containsKey(DataOptions.CURRENT_PRICE))
            .openPrice(requestParams.containsKey(DataOptions.OPEN_PRICE))
    .percentChange(requestParams.containsKey(DataOptions.PERCENTAGE_CHANGE))
        .volume(requestParams.containsKey(DataOptions.VOLUME));

            return options;
        }
}
```

Notice first that `PortfolioBroadcastEndpoint` is mapped to the URI template path /updates/{access-level} rather than an exact URI like all the endpoints you have looked at so far in the book. Next, notice that the `startUpdates()` method, which is the open event handler for this endpoint, has the method parameter

```
@PathParam("access-level") String accessLevel
```

which is asking for the value of the `access-level` path parameter produced by a match on this URI template path to be passed into this method. The first thing the `startUpdates()` method does is use the value of the `accessLevel` variable to create a `MemberLevel` object, which it will use to request updates from the source of the stock data in this application, the `StockDataSource` class. As you will see by browsing the rest of the source code for this application, the `MemberLevel` type is an enum type with values `MemberLevel.BRONZE`, `MemberLevel.SILVER`, and `MemberLevel.GOLD`. The second thing `startUpdates()` does is to build a `DataOptions` object based on the request parameters carried in the query string attached to the request URI the client sent to connect. The `DataOptions` object describes a list of the data fields that will be used to decide which fields to display in the output area on the web page. The client has formulated the query string based on which of the data field options has been checked in the Control Panel on the web page. Note that in the query strings in this example, the request parameters have no values, just names, because that is all the example needs. This means that the kinds of URIs the client is using to connect are similar to these:

```
ws://localhost:8080/portfolio/
            updates/bronze?current-price&open-price&percentage-change
ws://localhost:8080/portfolio/
            updates/silver?current-price&percentage-change
ws://localhost:8080/portfolio/
            updates/gold?current-price&open-price&percentage-change&volume
```

The `startUpdates()` method on the PortfolioBroadcastEndpoint class uses the `MemberLevel` and the `DataOptions` objects to create a `StockDataSource` object. The details of the implementation of the `StockDataSource` class are not particularly relevant to the topic of path mapping and processing the Java WebSocket API, so we will not dwell on them. The most pertinent facts about this object are that it will call `PortfolioBroadcastEndpoint` back when it has a new update on the stock information. It makes this callback with an object called a `PortfolioUpdate`, which holds all the stock information. Depending on the member level, `StockDataSource` will supply updates more or less frequently. Whenever the `PortfolioBroadcastEndpoint` gets a callback from the `StockDataSource` (in the form of a call to its `handleNewStockData()` method), it immediately sends the `PortfolioUpdate` object back to the client. You will notice from its `@ServerEndpoint` declaration, the `PortfolioBroadcastEndpoint` uses an encoder. This encoder, `PortfolioUpdateEncoder`, takes the stock information, the member level, and `DataOptions` and formats an HTML table containing the stock information, with only the data fields requested, and applies a color scheme and a disclaimer about the freshness of the data.

As a side note, you will notice that this is a type of endpoint that broadcasts updates to its clients on a schedule unrelated to any messages the clients are sending. In fact, as we noted, the JavaScript client in this case never actually sends the `PortfolioBroadcastEndpoint` endpoint a message at all. All such endpoints need a reference to the Session object in order to do this, so they will typically store the session object as an instance variable in the open handler method.

As a second side note, notice that `PortfolioBroadcastEndpoint` never deals with any display code. All the code that formats HTML sent back to the client is held in `PortfolioUpdateEncoder`. There are many design options in web applications for where to hold display code such as this (perhaps too many!), but certainly keeping it separate from the logic of the message processing in `PortfolioBroadcastEndpoint` likely makes it always a good choice.

Once the encoder has encoded the information, the WebSocket implementation sends the HTML update to the JavaScript client, which displays it and the circle is completed until either another update emanates from the `StockDataSource`, or the client changes something in the control panel or navigates away from the page.

# Query Strings vs. Path Parameters vs. WebSocket Messages

Even in this simple example, we are faced with some fundamental design choices about where to store the various parameters that define what type of information the client wants and how the client should receive it.

This application chose to use the request parameters sent in the query string to represent which data fields to send in the updates, essentially to define what information should be sent. It used the path parameter to define how the data should be sent: the member level path attribute was the key for the server endpoint to decide how often the updates should be sent and how it should be portrayed.

But the application could equally have defined a format of a WebSocket message that the client would send that contained all these pieces of qualifying information that helped the server endpoint structure the conversation.

So when do you choose to encode this kind of qualifying information in a message, in a collection of path parameters, or in a collection of request parameters contained in a query string?

As with many questions, there isn't really a clear answer that covers all applications. But here are four guidelines to think about as you decide.

### Guideline 1: How structured is the qualifying data you want to send?

If the qualifying data you want to send is at all structured beyond simple key value pairs, then it is hard to see how you could easily fit it into either path parameters or request parameters. If you have more than one level of information, you should probably consider inventing a message format so you can send it in a WebSocket message. However, if the qualifying data is a simple list of single-valued properties, then being able to have the Java WebSocket API parse out the values for you can be a big savings in design and implementation of message encoding and decoding code. If any of your qualifying data properties are multivalued, then because each request parameter can take multiple values, this approach may be a better fit than path parameters, which can only be single valued.

If, in the Portfolio application, you wanted to add parameters to govern how many decimal points you wanted the stock prices quoted in for both the current price and the opening price, that might be the point at which you would decide it would be time to create a message format to hold the qualifying data because defining such parameters would bring in a second level of structure to the data that would need to be carried in the query string.

However, this data in the Portfolio application is easily represented as key value pairs where the values are empty. In so doing, it avoids having to define a message format to carry the data completely. Instead of having to write decoding code, the application is able simply to use the parsing capabilities of the Java WebSocket API for the request and path parameters.

### Guideline 2: How often do you need or want to send the qualifying data?

If it is necessary in your application to update the qualifying information without bringing down the connection and establishing a new one each time, you will not be able to use the request and path parameters because they are sent only when the connection is first established.

### Guideline 3: How much data is there?

Although very long URIs can be formulated, web browsers impose an upper limit on the length of the URI they can cope with. For example, Internet Explorer has a maximum length of 2,048 characters for the URIs it will handle. This should be a factor in whether you decide to use either path parameters or the query string to this kind of application "metadata."

### Guideline 4: What other path mappings are in your application?

As you saw in some of the rules for path mapping in this chapter, once you have more than one endpoint in an application, there are some limitations in how you combine path mappings. If you have simple, flat qualifying information to convey at the time of opening a connection, the rules for path mapping may limit your options for using path parameters widely. However, because query strings are not part of the processing decisions for matching incoming URI to endpoints, the format of the query string you use is entirely unlimited by other endpoints in the application.

# Summary of WebSocket Path Mapping APIs

We'll end this chapter by summarizing the APIs relating to path mapping in the Java WebSocket API.

| API | Function |
|---|---|
| `ServerEndpointConfig.Builder public static`<br>`ServerEndpointConfig.Builder`<br>`create(Class<?> endpointClass, String path)` | Assigns the path value on creation (either relative URI or URI template) to the configuration object that will be used to deploy a programmatic endpoint. |
| `@ServerEndpoint`<br>`String value() attribute` | The annotation attribute used to define the path value (either relative URI or URI-template) for an annotated endpoint. |
| `ServerEndpointConfig`<br>`public String getPath()` | The path (relative URI or URI template) under which this endpoint is published. |
| `Session`<br>`public String getRequestURI()` | The URI relative to the web server root that the client used in establishing the connection. |
| `Session`<br>`public Map<String, String> getPathParameters()` | The key-value pairs produced when the client is connected to an endpoint that is published using a URI template. The keys are the name of the URI template variable; the values are the corresponding path segments in the client's request URI. |
| `Session`<br>`public String getQueryString()` | The query string portion of the request URI the client used to connect. |
| `Session`<br>`public Map<String, List<String>> getRequestParameterMap()` | Return the map of key to multiple value pairs extracted from the query string of the request URI the client used to connect. |

| API | Function |
|---|---|
| @PathParam<br>String value() attribute | Method parameter level annotation available for use in any annotated endpoint's lifecycle methods in order to extract a path parameter from a request URI when the endpoint is mapped to a URI template path. The value attribute indicates the name of the path parameter that is to be extracted. |

# Summary

This chapter examined all the options for publishing server WebSocket endpoints. We reviewed the mechanisms for assigning a path to an annotated and a programmatic endpoint. We examined both the mechanisms for publishing endpoints using exact URIs and URI templates. You learned the nine rules of path mapping in the Java WebSocket API that govern how the Java WebSocket API matches incoming URIs from client WebSocket endpoints as they attempt to connect to published endpoints in the WebSocket server. We ended the chapter by looking at an example application, the Portfolio application that puts some of these mechanisms to work, and discussed some of the design issues when deciding which mapping technique to use in an application.

# CHAPTER
## 7

# Securing WebSocket
Server Endpoints

Y ou may not want everyone to have access to a WebSocket endpoint you publish, and for those that do have access, you may want to tailor its interactions to suit the person who has access to it. If you are using a WebSocket on a social networking site that broadcasts your location on a map, you may not want the map containing your location to be seen by just anyone. If a WebSocket endpoint sends out breaking news updates, you may well wish that it tailored the news to those topics in which you have shown interest in the past.

The security model in the Java WebSocket API largely focuses on the main deployment setup for WebSockets: a JavaScript WebSocket client running in a web page accessing a Java WebSocket API server endpoint running in a web server. This chapter looks at the various mechanisms in the Java WebSocket API for selectively gating access to Java WebSocket server endpoints to particular users. We will mostly focus on how WebSocket endpoints running on a server and accessed by a browser client can be published to meet a variety of privacy constraints.

Those of you who are very familiar with the security for Java Servlets in the Java EE platform should find the security model for the Java WebSocket API relatively straightforward to understand because it builds on the declarative security model of the web layer in the Java EE platform. We will start with some basic security concepts to use as a foundation for understanding the model.

# Security Concepts

Let's start by looking at our basic deployment scenario: someone using a web browser to access a resource on a web server (see Figure 7-1).

In the picture, the user is initiating a request from a web page loaded into the browser for a resource that is protected by the security model on the server. Before the request can be fulfilled, the server's security model has to consider the following three questions.

- *Who is asking for the resource?* If the user has not logged into the server, the request is anonymous. It may be that the security model allows anonymous access to the resource, or it may be that the server has to know the identity of the user requesting the resource in order answer the next question.

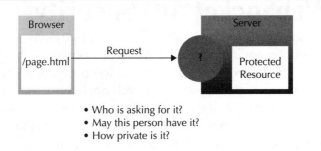

**FIGURE 7-1.**   *The three security questions*

■ *May this person have it?* If the server does not allow anonymous access to the resource, then it will hold somewhere the information necessary to determine if this particular user is allowed access to the resource or not. Once the server has made this determination, the server will need to consider the next question.

■ *How private is its data?* The server may have decided that the data the resource yields in response to the request must be delivered back to the client in such a way that there is a level of guarantee that the information has not been altered en route. Or the server may wish to ensure, to some level of certainty, that anyone intercepting the data it sends from the resource to the client cannot read it.

The processes of determining the answers to these questions are more commonly known as

■ **Authentication**   The process of communicating the identity of a user making a request

■ **Authorization**   The process of granting or denying access to a resource

■ **Guaranteeing data privacy**   The determination of how private the communication channel used to transmit data between the resource and the client is

# Java WebSocket API Security

The Java WebSocket API contains a number of features that allow you to configure a security model for a web application containing the WebSocket endpoint you want to protect. It allows you to configure a variety of authentication schemes for access to the web application, it allows you to grant or deny access to specific classes of user of your web application, and it allows you to indicate what level of data privacy you wish to require for access to WebSocket endpoints in the web application.

The Java WebSocket API contains a number of API calls that allow you to access aspects of the security model from a running application, and also allows you to build your own application-specific security features into your application, should the features built into the Java WebSocket API not be sufficient for the needs of the application.

Of course, every good security model has many more features outside the core three we have just described, such as auditing, non-repudiation, and interoperability. Every implementation of the Java WebSocket API will have some level of support for these features, but the level of support is likely to differ from implementation to implementation. We will focus on the three core features because they are supported in a standard way by the Java WebSocket API and because they cover the security needs of the majority of Java WebSocket applications.

Let's start by taking a look at how to configure authentication in a Java WebSocket application.

## Authentication

If you plan on allowing only authenticated users to use your WebSocket endpoint, then you have a choice of schemes when the Java WebSocket API is running in a Java EE implementation, as you are about to see in the subsections that follow.

### Basic Authentication

This is the simplest of HTTP-based authentication schemes. The client sends the username and password pair (usually known as the credentials) encoded in an HTTP header. The client may either send this preemptively or in reaction to a challenge that the server issues if the client sends an unauthenticated request. This is a good scheme to use in a WebSocket application if you need a kind of sign-in and to know which user is accessing the WebSocket. This is useful in applications where you wish to tailor the content to the user because you already know something about them, but you do not necessarily need a strong security scheme to protect the data you are sending or receiving. Because the credentials in the HTTP Basic scheme are sent un-encrypted, they are very vulnerable to being intercepted and decoded. It is for this reason that many web applications that do wish to protect the credentials and the application data choose to use HTTP Basic authentication over only an encrypted or private connection.

Browsers typically use a basic modal username password dialog to retrieve the user credentials, so the user experience, while simple, is not easy to customize.

## Form-Based Authentication

Form-based authentication is a mechanism that defines a set of request parameters that signify a user's username and password, which are encoded in a special `<form>` element in the web page. Like basic authentication, the credentials are sent unencrypted, so this suits the same class of applications. The main difference between form authentication and HTTP Basic authentication is that the look and placement of the login form is customizable, so it suits applications that are more conscious of the user experience.

## Digest Authentication

Digest authentication is a mechanism that gathers a username–password combination from the client and sends it in a protected form to the server for verification. Because the credentials are sent in a protected form, this is inherently a more secure form of authentication than either HTTP Basic or form-based authentication. However, because there is no way for the client to know it is sending the credential information to the correct server, and not one masquerading as such, it is not the most secure form of encryption.

## Client Certificate Authentication

Client-certificated authentication is a process by which the server and, optionally, the client authenticate one another using a digital certificate, which acts as a kind of encrypted passport that verifies the agent's identity.

The process is inherently more secure than either HTTP Basic or form-based authentication because the credentials are always transferred using HTTP over SSL and because the client is able to verify the server identity.

Unfortunately, none of these mechanisms are reliably invoked by directly attempting an unauthenticated handshake from a JavaScript WebSocket endpoint. While the WebSocket protocol theoretically allows implementations to insert their own authentication interactions within the opening handshake, implementations of the WebSocket protocol do not typically do so yet. However, when a browser attempts the opening handshake of a JavaScript WebSocket from within a web page, the opening handshake it issues carries the authentication context of the enclosing web page. What this means is that, in order to access a WebSocket endpoint that requires authentication from client-side JavaScript WebSocket, you have to ensure that the web page holding the JavaScript WebSocket has been authenticated with a user identity that is authorized to access the endpoint.

As motivation for picking an authentication scheme for your application, you will need to authenticate your users if you wish to limit access to either any of your WebSocket endpoints to known users, or any subset thereof, or the WebSocket endpoints in the application need to access the user identity at runtime, perhaps to do some kind of application level security, or simply to display a username.

Once you have decided which scheme you wish to use, configuring it is relatively easy: You specify it in the deployment descriptor of the WAR file in which your endpoints are packaged. The key element to include in the deployment descriptor is the `<login-config>` element. The table that follows shows its sub-elements.

| Element Name | Value | Purpose |
| --- | --- | --- |
| auth-method | BASIC, FORM, DIGEST, or CLIENT-CERT | Defines the authentication scheme |
| realm-name | Name of the user realm used for basic authentication | Defines which server realm will be used to verify the basic authentication credentials |

| Element Name | Value | Purpose |
|---|---|---|
| `form-login-config` | Sub-elements `login-page` and `error-page` | For form login only, defines the relative location within the web application of the page containing the login form, and the page to which the user is redirected if the login fails |

## Examples

Here are some excerpts of web.xml files that specify each of the four types of authentication you can use for WebSocket applications.

For basic authentication, including this snippet of XML under the top level web-app element of the web.xml will configure an application to receive an HTTP Basic authentication challenge when attempting to access a protected resource. The server will verify the credentials the client sends by matching them in the server's `file` authentication realm.

**Listing:** *Basic Authentication*

```
<login-config>
    <auth-method>BASIC</auth-method>
    <realm-name>file</realm-name>
</login-config>
```

You can see how to specify your application use form authentication in the next example. If you include the following XML under the top-level web-app element of your web.xml, the server will redirect any unauthenticated requests to protected resources within the web application to the login.html page located at the root of the web application's URI namespace.

**Listing:** *Form login Authentication*

```
<login-config>
    <auth-method>FORM</auth-method>
    <form-login-config>
```

```
    <form-login-page>/login.html</form-login-page>
    <form-error-page>/error.html</form-error-page>
    </form-login-config>
</login-config>
```

Now, if the `login.html` page contains an HTML form of the shape shown in the next example, then the form submission will post request parameters named `j_username` and `j_password` containing the values of the username and password the user enters to a specially reserved resource named `j_security_check` on the server that processes the authentication request. Should the authentication succeed, the user will be redirected to the protected resource he requested in the first place. If the authentication fails, the user will be redirected to the `error.html` page, which was specified in the `form-login-config` element and which is located at the root of the web application's URI space.

**Listing:** *A Login <form>*

```
<form method=POST action="j_security_check">
        User ID
    <input type="text" size="10" name="j_username"> <br>
        Password
    <input type="password" size="10" name="j_password">
    <input type="submit" name="login" value="Login">
</form>
```

To specify that your application use digest authentication, include the XML shown in the following code listing under the top-level web-app element in your `web.xml` deployment descriptor file.

**Listing:** *Digest Authentication*

```
<login-config>
    <auth-method>DIGEST</auth-method>
</login-config>
```

This means that whenever a user tries to access a protected resource in your application, he will face a digest authentication challenge.

Finally, the following code listing shows the `login-config` element you would need to include in your web application if you would like the server to initiate a client-certificate challenge when an unauthenticated user of the web application attempts to access a protected resource.

**Listing:**   *Client Certificate Authentication*

```
<login-config>
    <auth-method>CLIENT-CERT</auth-method>
</login-config>
```

If you use this method of authentication, you will need to ensure that you have installed a verified client certificate that the server will trust and recognize is from you.

The ability to specify an authentication scheme for the web pages that contain the client-side JavaScript WebSocket endpoints that wish to access protected server-side Java WebSocket endpoints isn't of any use unless you know how to protect those server-side endpoints in the first place. So we turn to the language of *authentication* in Java WebSocket applications.

# Authorization

Authorization is the process by which the WebSocket implementation decides if a particular user is permitted access to a particular endpoint. The Java EE platform uses a level of indirection in defining users called a *user role,* or simply a *role*. A role is a kind of abstraction of a user that allows authorization rules to be set up in the application without the developer having to hardwire actual usernames in the application configuration.

When an authenticated opening handshake request comes in to the server, the server must carry out three things in order to decide whether it will grant access to the endpoint the request is for.

First, the server must determine to which role or roles the authenticated user belongs. This information is not part of the standard configuration defined by the Java WebSocket API, and so will vary from WebSocket implementation to WebSocket implementation. In the Glassfish 4.0 application server, you can make the association between the user and the roles in a deployment descriptor specific to Glassfish called the `glassfish.xml` file that you co-package with the WAR file containing your endpoints, but other application servers use different schemes.

Second, once the server knows the roles to which the opening handshake request belongs, it decides by looking at the application's web deployment descriptor (the `web.xml` file co-packaged in the WAR file). You will look at some specific examples of this in the material that follows, but for now, it is enough to know that for a given URI (the URI of the opening handshake) the `web.xml`'s security constraints contain all the information necessary to determine which roles are allowed access to that URI.

Finally, of course, as you have seen, the WebSocket endpoint is mapped to a path in its own configuration mechanism, either using a `ServerEndpointConfig` for programmatic endpoints or in the value attribute of the `ServerEndpoint` annotation for annotated endpoints.

With these three pieces of information, the server can then decide for a given user and opening handshake request URI whether any of the roles to which the user belongs are allowed access to the URI.

This mechanism and the locations of the configuration information necessary to make this determination are summarized in Figure 7-2.

Let's take a look at the configuration syntax in web.xml for restricting access on an endpoint to a set of user roles.

The element to use is the `security-constraint` element. To define the URI or URIs to which you wish to restrict access, you will need to define

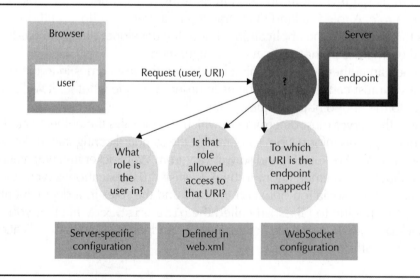

**FIGURE 7-2.** *Determining authorization*

a `web-resource-collection`, sub-element which has the following sub-elements:

| web-resource-collection Sub Element | Multiplicity | Value |
|---|---|---|
| `web-resource-collection-name` | Single | Optional text name of this collection of URIs for display in tools |
| `description` | Single | An optional text description of this collection of URIs for display in tools |
| `url-pattern` | Multiple | A path designation indicating a URI or group of URIs |
| `http-method` | Multiple | The HTTP method (GET, POST, etc.) used to access the resource |

You have a choice of how you specify the paths in the `url-pattern` elements you use:

- **Exact path**  This is a path relative to the context root of the web application—for example, `/websockets/myendpoint`.

- **Wildcard**  This is a path that defines a group of URLs, relative to the context root of the web application. For example, `/websockets/*` would indicate all URIs starting with `websockets`.

- **Filename ending**  This is a `url-pattern` that looks for a particular endpoint pattern in a URI. For example, if you decided to map all the endpoints in your application to paths that ended in `.ws` such as `/banking/advertisingendpoint.ws`, `/marketnewsendpoint.ws`, the `url-pattern .ws` would mean both the endpoint paths.

The `http-method` element is not needed for WebSocket endpoints; all opening handshake requests are GET requests, and omitting the element covers all possible HTTP methods. If you do list HTTP methods other that GET in this method for some reason, the WebSocket implementation will not count them as part of your security constraint for WebSocket endpoints. So it's best to leave out this element, unless you are additionally using this syntax to protect other web components in your web application using the same security constraint.

Once you have set up one or more web-resource collections in your security constraint, you will need to indicate which roles are allowed access to the URI specified in the web-resource-collection. To do that, simply append a list of `auth-constraint` elements to the security-constraint, each of which contains the name of the role to which you would like to grant access. Any role names you list here must already be declared in a `security-role` element in the web.xml.

## Examples

Let's take a look at some examples. Suppose we have a web application containing a web page and a server endpoint. The web page is called `home.html`, and the endpoint is mapped to `/endpoint`. The `home.html` web page contains a JavaScript client WebSocket endpoint that will access the server endpoint. We wish to allow only users who are in the `customer` role to be able to access the web page and endpoint. Because this is a web application that does not require the strictest security policy, we are happy to authenticate users using the basic authentication scheme. The following code listing presents the security snippet from the `web.xml` file we need to secure the web application to that policy.

**Listing:** *A Security Constraint Example*

```
<security-constraint>
    <display-name>WebSocket Constraint</display-name>
    <web-resource-collection>
        <web-resource-name>web page and WebSocket</web-resource-name>
        <description>This restricts access to the web page and the
                     WebSocket it will try to access</description>
        <url-pattern>/home.jsp</url-pattern>
        <url-pattern>/endpoint</url-pattern>
    </web-resource-collection>
    <auth-constraint>
        <description/>
        <role-name>customer</role-name>
    </auth-constraint>
</security-constraint>
<login-config>
    <auth-method>BASIC</auth-method>
    <realm-name>file</realm-name>
</login-config>
```

```
<security-role>
    <role-name>customer</role-name>
</security-role>
<security-role>
    <role-name>administrator</role-name>
</security-role>
```

Now when a new user tries to access the home.html page, the server will issue an HTTP Basic authentication challenge because the home.html page is only allowed to be accessed by users who are in the customer role, as you can see from the security-constraint in the preceding example. Notice that the web application has two roles, customer and administrator. If the challenge meets with success, the user is able to access the home.html web page. If the user causes the home.html page to attempt to connect to the WebSocket server endpoint mapped to /endpoint from the JavaScript client endpoint embedded in the web page, the server will intercept the opening handshake issued by the browser on behalf of the client endpoint. The opening handshake request will carry the authentication context of the user (unless the user logged out in the meantime, or the session timed out), which the server will use to verify access to the /endpoint URI. If the opening handshake carries the correct authentication context, the opening handshake will proceed, and the connection will be established.

Note that unauthenticated opening handshakes issued in any way by the client to this protected WebSocket server endpoint will meet with failure. Specifically, any unauthenticated opening handshake will receive an HTTP 401 (Not Authorized) HTTP response in place of a successful opening handshake response.

You can see the sequence of steps, reading from top to bottom, in Figure 7-3.

# Private Communication

In order to protect the data exchanged between WebSocket endpoints, the syntax of the web.xml deployment descriptor allows you to mark portions of the URI space as one of the following:

- **INTEGRAL**   This means that no third party should be able to tamper with the data as it is being exchanged by changing it during transmission.

- **CONFIDENTIAL**   This means that no third party should be able to tamper or even read the data as it is being exchanged.

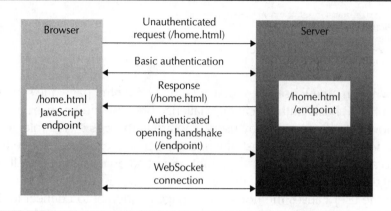

**FIGURE 7-3.** *Authorization interactions*

Most application servers interpret either option as meaning they should only allow access to the resource—in our case, to a WebSocket endpoint on the server—using a secure connection, i.e., WebSockets over SSL, or `wss`. There are two things to specify to ensure private communication between a JavaScript WebSocket and a server side WebSocket written using the Java WebSocket API.

First, the client must specify `wss://` in its opening handshake and use the SSL port of the web server hosting the WebSockets. The following is a quick example of the JavaScript code to create a WebSocket object that will connect using `wss://`:

```
var myWebSocket = new WebSocket("wss://localhost:8181/
                               SecureApp/secure-endpoint")
```

In this case, the server uses port 8181 for SSL connections.

Second, the web application containing the server WebSocket endpoint needs to specify that it may only be accessed over a private WebSocket connection. To do this, you must define a `security-constraint` with a `url-pattern` that matches the path of the endpoint you wish to communicate privately, and add to it a `user-data-constraint`. The table that follows shows the sub-elements of `user-data-constraint`.

| Subelements of user-data-constraint | Value | Purpose |
|---|---|---|
| `description` | text | An optional text description of the constraint when looking at the deployment descriptor in a tool |
| `transport-guarantee` | NONE, INTEGRAL, or CONFIDENTIAL | The level of privacy defined by the constraint. NONE, the default, is interpreted as no private communication is needed; INTEGRAL and CONFIDENTIAL as access only by `wss`. |

For example, you can adapt the example to illustrate authorization by adding the following `user-data-constraint` to the `security-constraint` to mean that both the page and the endpoint within it can only be accessed by authenticated users in the customer role using `wss`, rather than `ws`.

**Listing:**   *CONFIDENTIAL Connection*

```
<user-data-constraint>
      <transport-guarantee>CONFIDENTIAL</transport-guarantee>
</user-data-constraint>
```

Therefore, now you would need to alter the URL used by the JavaScript WebSocket to use `wss` instead of `ws` to ensure both ends of the connection agree that the connection should be private.

If you wish to communicate from a web page to an endpoint using `wss`, typically you will only be able to do so in a browser that has already established an HTTPS connection with your web application. What this means in real terms is that if you have a web page containing a JavaScript WebSocket endpoint that wishes to connect using `wss` to a server-side Java WebSocket endpoint, you will need to ensure there is a `security-constraint` for both the JavaScript endpoint *and* the web page holding it that has `user-data-constraint` that is set to either INTEGRAL or CONFIDENTIAL. This is similar to the situation you already encountered with authentication; the web page holding the client WebSocket must already be authenticated if you wish it to access a server-side Java WebSocket that requires authentication.

# Java WebSocket Security APIs

There are various APIs that you can access at runtime to give your application a view into the security model you have set up in the containing web application deployment descriptor.

## Security Information Available on the Session Object

It is often useful to access the authenticated user of the connection to the WebSocket. This information is available from the `Session` object using the following method call:

```
public Principal getUserPrincipal()
```

This returns a `java.security.Principal` object representing the user, from which you can obtain the name, and by further examining the actual sub-type, more information about the user and her associated credentials. If the connection was not authenticated, then the method returns `null`. This method is useful for a number of things, from embedding the user's name in WebSocket messages that your endpoint sends, to building your own authorization checks into the application rather than relying on the security-constraint mechanism provided for you in the web container, which we examined earlier in this chapter.

From the `Session` object, you can also ascertain whether the connection is private or not, that is to say, if the WebSocket connection is encrypted or not. This information is available using the following call:

```
public boolean isSecure()
```

## Security Information Available on the HandshakeRequest

As you know from Chapter 4, you can intercept the opening handshake request in a server WebSocket endpoint. This is done by subclassing the `ServerEndpointConfig.Configurator` class and overriding its

```
public void modifyHandshake(ServerEndpointConfig sec,
        HandshakeRequest request,  HandshakeResponse response)
```

method, and by linking the endpoint to the configurator class either using the `@ServerEndpoint`'s `configurator` attribute for annotated endpoints, or by setting the configurator on the `ServerEndpointConfig` instance you create when deploying a programmatic endpoint.

When you do this, from your `modifyHandshake()` method, you have access to the `HandshakeRequest` object. This is the same method as you already saw on the `Session` object:

```
public Principal getUserPrincipal()
```

Additionally, the `HandshakeRequest` has the method

```
public boolean isUserInRole(String rolename)
```

The purpose of this method is to allow you to determine whether the authenticated user making the opening handshake request is a member of the role name you pass in. For example, if you list a `security-role` of `customer` in the web.xml deployment descriptor in the web application containing an endpoint, from the `HandshakeRequest` object that you obtain when a client attempts to connect to the endpoint, you can determine if the client user identity is part of the `customer` role. This can be useful if you wish to provide different levels of interaction from your endpoint depending on which role each active user belongs to, or if you wish to provide your own security model as part of the application rather than relying on the security constraint mechanism provided for you in the web container. If the client has made an unauthenticated connection to the endpoint, then this method always returns `false`, as it does if you pass in a role that is not known in the web application.

Our example application for this chapter will make use of these security APIs, but before we leave this topic, the following is a summary of all the security-related APIs in the Java WebSocket API.

| API Object | API Call | Purpose |
| --- | --- | --- |
| Session | `Principal getUserPrincipal()` | Obtain the authenticated user of the connection. |
| Session | `boolean isSecure()` | Establish if the current connection is encrypted. |
| HandshakeRequest | `boolean isUserInRole( String rolename)` | Establish if the current authenticated user is in the role supplied. |

| API Object | API Call | Purpose |
|---|---|---|
| HandshakeRequest | Principal getUserPrincipal() | Obtain the authenticated user attempting to open the connection. |

# Stock Account Application

We will round out our look at the Java WebSocket API security model with an example. The Stock Account application is a web application that is accessed through a browser client. On the main entry page, you will find a banner containing market information about the prices of a number of companies and equities, as you can see in Figure 7-4.

When you log in, you are asked to provide a username and password, and you are taken to an account screen. As you can see in Figure 7-5, you still have the banner, but the financial information is more up-to-date and updates more frequently. In addition, you can see a listing of the current positions of your stock portfolio. You will also see that the current market value of your portfolio is being constantly updated as new market data about the equities you own becomes available. From this page you can log out of the application and return to the original main entry screen.

Notice that both the entry page and the account page are only accessible through HTTPS. And notice, of course, that you have to provide a username and password in order to access the account page. This application comes preconfigured to run on the Glassfish 4.0 application server with two users: Alexander and Jesse. You'll notice that you get different levels of service depending on whether you are logged in as Alexander or whether you are logged in as Jesse.

Inside the application there are two server-side endpoints, with their class names and path mappings shown in the following table.

| Endpoint Class | URI Mapping |
|---|---|
| AccountEndpoint | /account/info |
| PortfolioBroadcastEndpoint | /banner/{secure-access} |

The PortfolioBroadcastEndpoint should already be somewhat familiar. It is based on the endpoint of the same name that you saw in the Portfolio application from the previous chapter. Its purpose now, as it was

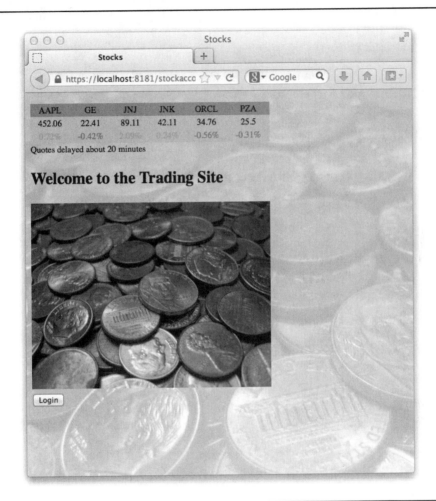

**FIGURE 7-4.**   *Entering the Stock Account application*

then, is to send notifications of new stock prices, as a kind of stock ticker function. It gives more frequent updates and the data is fresher the higher the `MemberLevel` in the application. You'll see in a minute how the member level is determined. The `AccountEndpoint` powers the updates to the account information, taking the current market data and calculating, based on the user's current positions in each equity, the current market value of the user's holding

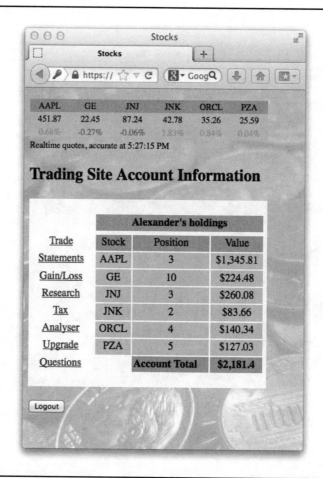

**FIGURE 7-5.** *A Gold Level user's account information*

in each one. Again, `AccountEndpoint` uses the `MemberLevel` to give differentiated levels of service.

Let's take a look at the deployment descriptor for this application.

**Listing:** *Stock Account Deployment Descriptor*

```
<?xml version="1.0" encoding="UTF-8"?>
<web-app version="3.0" xmlns="http://java.sun.com/xml/ns/
javaee" xmlns:xsi="http://www.w3.org/2001/XMLSchema-instance"
xsi:schemaLocation="http://java.sun.com/xml/ns/javaee http://java.sun.com/xml/
ns/javaee/web-app_3_0.xsd">
```

```
<session-config>
    <session-timeout>
        30
    </session-timeout>
</session-config>
<security-constraint>
    <display-name> login access</display-name>
    <web-resource-collection>
        <web-resource-name>Account Info</web-resource-name>
        <url-pattern>/index.jsp</url-pattern>
    </web-resource-collection>
    <user-data-constraint>
        <transport-guarantee>CONFIDENTIAL</transport-guarantee>
    </user-data-constraint>
</security-constraint>
<security-constraint>
    <display-name>customer_access</display-name>
    <web-resource-collection>
        <web-resource-name>Account Info</web-resource-name>
        <url-pattern>/account.jsp</url-pattern>
        <url-pattern>/account/info</url-pattern>
        <url-pattern>/banner/secure</url-pattern>
    </web-resource-collection>
    <auth-constraint>
        <role-name>customer</role-name>
        <role-name>premium_customer</role-name>
    </auth-constraint>
    <user-data-constraint>
        <transport-guarantee>CONFIDENTIAL</transport-guarantee>
    </user-data-constraint>
</security-constraint>
<login-config>
    <auth-method>BASIC</auth-method>
    <realm-name>file</realm-name>
</login-config>
<security-role>
    <role-name>customer</role-name>
</security-role>
<security-role>
    <role-name>premium_customer</role-name>
</security-role>
</web-app>
```

The first thing to notice is that the Stock Account application uses two
security constraints that restrict access to the web pages and to the two
endpoints. The first security constraint in web.xml places a condition of
private communication on accessing the `index.jsp` home page. This
ensures that you can only access `index.jsp` using HTTPS. The second
security constraint places an authorization control on `account.jsp`
and the `AccountEndpoint` endpoint. This allows only those users who
are in the roles of `customer` or `premium_customer` to access those
resources. You will also see that the same security constraint restricts

access to the URI /banner/secure, which is a potential match on the PortfolioBroadcastEndpoint endpoint, to users in those same roles. This ensures that any user attempting to access the account page, or the AccountEndpoint endpoint, or the PortfolioBroadcastEndpoint via the path /banner/secure, must be authenticated and belong to the correct role. Looking at the login-config element of web.xml, you'll see that the authentication method is HTTP Basic, but because the index.jsp page that causes the login by attempting to open the account.jsp is itself only accessible over HTTPS, the HTTP basic authentication information is being transmitted over an encrypted connection. This is usually a good habit to get into, unless you are treating authentication very loosely.

You will notice that when the entry page index.jsp accesses the PortfolioBroadcastEndpoint, it does so using the URI /banner/nouser instead of /banner/secure as the account page does. This means, of course, that because index.jsp has no authorization control placed on it (just the user-data-constraint), you do not need to be logged in to be able to see the stock ticker information it produces at the top of the page.

Each of the endpoints uses a custom configurator in order to figure out the MemberLevel for each user. The MemberLevel is used at the heart of the application in order to determine the level of service and display scheme for the account page. Let's take a look at how this is done. In the MemberLevelConfigurator class, you will see below that we have overridden the modifyHandshake() method.

**Listing:** *The MemberLevelConfigurator*

```
public class MemberLevelConfigurator extends
                ServerEndpointConfig.Configurator {
    public static String CUSTOMER = "customer";
    public static String PREMIUM_CUSTOMER = "premium_customer";
    public static String MEMBER_LEVEL = "MemberLevel";

    public void modifyHandshake(ServerEndpointConfig sec,
                HandshakeRequest request,
                HandshakeResponse response) {
        MemberLevel ml = null;
        if (request.isUserInRole(CUSTOMER)) {
            ml = MemberLevel.SILVER;
        } else if (request.isUserInRole(PREMIUM_CUSTOMER)) {
            ml = MemberLevel.GOLD;
        } else {
            ml = MemberLevel.BRONZE;
```

```
        }
        sec.getUserProperties().put(MEMBER_LEVEL, ml);
    }

}
```

You can see in the listing that this method is implemented using current user's membership of his user role to determine the level of access. Our user Alexander is a member of the `premier_customer` role, so he will be granted a gold level membership, as you saw earlier. Our user Jesse is a member of the `customer` role, but not the `premier_customer` role, so he pays a lower service fee; he will be granted a silver level membership, as you can see in Figure 7-6.

The implementation of modifyHandshake() in the `MemberLevelConfigurator` inserts the `MemberLevel` into the `ServerEndpointConfig` object.

Both endpoints use the `MemberLevelConfigurator`, as you can see from the class level WebSocket annotation, for example, for the `AccountEndpoint`:

---

**Listing:**   *Using the MemberLevelConfigurator*

```
@ServerEndpoint(
    value="/account/info",
    encoders={AccountUpdateEncoder.class},
    configurator=MemberLevelConfigurator.class
)
```

and in the `@OnOpen` method for the `AccountEndpoint`:

---

**Listing:**   *AccountEndpoint OnOpen Handler*

```
@OnOpen
public void startAccess(Session session, EndpointConfig ec)
    this.session = session;
    MemberLevel memberLevel = (MemberLevel)
  ec.getUserProperties().get(MemberLevelConfigurator.MEMBER_LEVEL);
    DataOptions options = (
            new DataOptions()).currentPrice(true).percentChange(true);
    this.account = new Account(session.getUserPrincipal(), memberLevel);
    this.dataSource = new StockDataSource(options, memberLevel);
    this.dataSource.addStockDataSourceListener(this);
    this.dataSource.start();
}
```

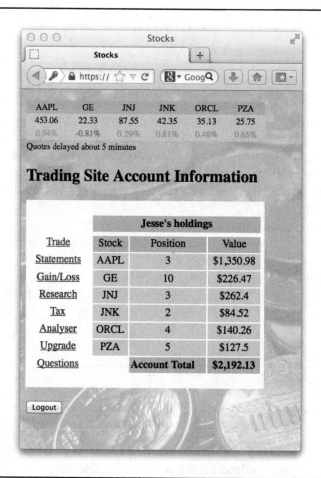

**FIGURE 7-6.** *A silver-level user's account information*

It is easy to see that the MemberLevel set by the MemberLevelConfigurator is retrieved here in order to set up the level of service from the data source that powers the market data updates.

The PortfolioBroadcastEndpoint similarly uses the MemberLevelConfigurator to determine its MemberLevel from the authenticated account information page. If the

`PortfolioBroadcastEndpoint` is accessed on an unauthenticated connection, as it is from the entry page `index.jsp`, then the user `Principal` object is `null`, and the `isUserInRole()` call used in the `MemberLevelConfigurator` always returns false, and you end up here with the lowest bronze level of service.

To summarize, this application uses the declarative security model to do the following:

■ Restrict all access to the endpoints to being over only encrypted connections

■ Restrict certain forms of access to its WebSocket endpoints to only certain authenticated users

■ Allow open access to one of the endpoints to unauthenticated users

Using some of the runtime Java WebSocket security APIs, we can interrogate the security model in order to differentiate the WebSocket activity depending on who is accessing the application.

# Summary

In this chapter, you learned how the web container's declarative security model can be used to restrict access to Java WebSocket server endpoints just to certain users. You learned the available methods of authenticating the identity of a user attempting to access a Java WebSocket server endpoint, and you learned how to ensure that Java WebSocket server endpoints can be accessed exclusively over encrypted connections. You learned about the runtime access Java WebSocket developers have to the encrypted state of the connection and to the identity of the authenticated client. Finally, you looked at the Stock Account application that applied the security model to a brokerage account containing valuable personal data and which provided tiered service levels depending on the user.

# CHAPTER
## 8

# WebSockets in the
# Java EE Platform

The Java WebSocket API is a standard part of the Java EE 7 platform, and is therefore available to all developers using an application server that supports the Java EE 7 APIs. So far in this book, we have focused on applications that just use the Java WebSocket API and no other APIs, except for some commonly used libraries from the Java SE platform. While this has allowed us to look in detail at all the important aspects of using the Java WebSocket API, many real-world WebSocket endpoints will be part of a larger enterprise application that has access to a wide variety of services and other technologies. In particular, given the origins of the WebSocket protocol as a solution for various forms of web application polling, and given the high level of support for the WebSocket protocol in web browsers, it is likely to be common to see WebSockets as part of a larger web application.

Therefore, this book would not be complete without some guidance as to how to write Java EE and web applications that incorporate WebSockets. There are already many books devoted to explaining how to use all of the Java APIs and components in the Java EE platform, and this is not one of them! So this chapter devotes some attention to the key topics of how to connect Java WebSocket endpoints with other web components in the web container, and how to connect Java WebSocket endpoints to Enterprise Java Beans. With these two connections as a starting point, you should be in a good position to apply your knowledge of all the other Java EE technologies to expand the reach and power of your Java WebSocket endpoints.

# The Role of Java WebSockets in the Java EE Platform

The Java EE platform (see Figure 8-1) shows the role of the Java WebSocket API in the web container.

The Java EE platform is home to two server-side containers: the web container and the EJB container. Both containers host and manage developer-created components. The web container hosts Java Servlets and a family of technologies that build on the Java Servlet model such as JavaServer Pages and JavaServer Faces, in addition to WebService endpoints, and, of course, WebSocket endpoints. The EJB container is home to a variety of flavors of Enterprise JavaBeans. Both server containers employ and make available to developers a variety of services. These include JDBC and Java Persistence for

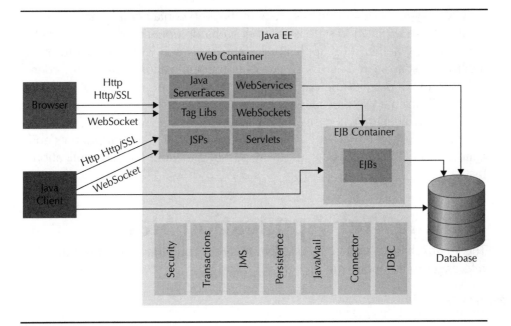

**FIGURE 8-1.**   *The Java EE platform architecture*

reading and writing application data to an external database, the JavaMessage
Service for reliable inter-app server messaging, various security services,
a transaction manager, and JavaMail. Typical Java EE applications hold a
number of web components, perhaps some EJB components, interacting
with a database either directly from the web components, or through the EJB
components. Users access these Java EE applications through a browser client,
or perhaps a rich client application of some kind, including a Java or JavaFX
rich client application. Browser interactions occur over HTTP and WebSocket
connections engaging web components that in turn engage EJB components
or the data layer, encrypted or open. Rich client application interactions may
occur over these same web protocols, too, engaging the web components
in the application. Alternatively, the Java EE platform includes a managed
container for client applications called the Application Client Container, which
allows direct communication to EJB components, in addition to the option of
communication with the web layer through web protocols.

Given WebSocket endpoint's place in the web container, it is natural to want to share application state with other web components in the same web application, whether it be application state associated with one client, or application state shared across all clients of the application. Equally, in order to interact with pre-existing components in the EJB layer, it is natural to want to call EJBs from a WebSocket endpoint.

These two central use cases will be the focus of our examination here: once a WebSocket endpoint can share data with other web components and interact with EJB components, it is truly part of the wider Java EE application that contains it.

# Sharing Web Application State

The key to sharing application state in the web container is in obtaining references to the following objects:

```
javax.servlet.ServletContext
javax.servlet.http.HttpSession
```

The `HttpSession` object represents a sequence of HTTP interactions from the same HTTP client to a web application. This means that the same user making a sequence of HTTP requests from a browser client, for example, will be associated with the same instance of the `HttpSession`. This is provided that the user doesn't wait too long between interactions, and provided that no one decides to terminate the session between requests. Web containers offer more than one mechanism to support the validity of an `HttpSession` in the web container. They use cookies where the client supports and allows them, and a technique called *URL rewriting* to track session state in the query string of the URIs used in the web application.

Because all WebSocket connections begin with the opening handshake, and because the opening handshake is an HTTP interaction, each WebSocket `Session` object is related to the `HttpSession` object that was initiated or already in place during the opening handshake that established it. This means that from every WebSocket endpoint running inside a web application, there is an `HttpSession` object that it is related to: the one in place for its opening handshake.

In more practical terms, any WebSocket connection initiated from a JavaScript WebSocket endpoint in a web page is related to the same `HttpSession` object created when the page was loaded. Suppose you have a web application consisting of a web page containing three JavaScript WebSocket client endpoints and Java WebSocket server endpoints. Suppose that the JavaScript client endpoints connect to the Java WebSocket server endpoints; then, each time a user downloaded the web page and caused the WebSockets to connect, you would have an HttpSession associated with three separate WebSocket Sessions. In Figure 8-2, you can see this arrangement, with two users using the web application.

Now, the HttpSession object holds a dictionary that developers may use to hold application data, which is a very useful feature. Naturally, because there is one HttpSession instance per user of the application, this application data is associated with the user. The dictionary is accessed with the methods shown in the listing that follows.

**Listing:** *User Attributes on the HttpSession*

```
public Object getAttribute(String name)
public Enumeration<String> getAttributeNames()
public void setAttribute(String name, Object value)
```

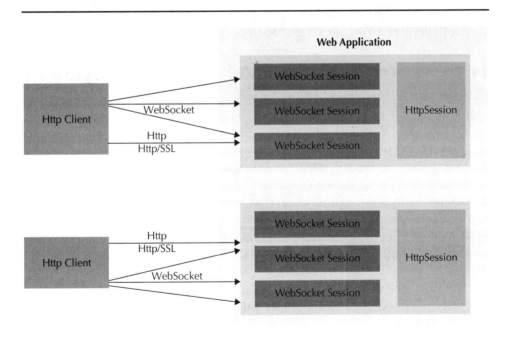

**FIGURE 8-2.** *Relationship between WebSocket Sessions and HttpSessions at opening handshake*

This makes it a very useful shared object for any component that has access to it. All Java Servlet and Java Servlet–based technologies have access to the `HttpSession` object, so they are able to share application state associated with a particular user.

Fortunately, Java WebSocket endpoints can also get access to the `HttpSession` object associated with their WebSocket `Sessions` in order to share application data associated with a particular user with other web components. They can do this by intercepting the opening handshake with a custom `ServletEndpointConfig.Configurator` and overriding the

```
public void modifyHandshake(ServerEndpointConfig sec,
                                HandshakeRequest request,
                                HandshakeResponse response)
```

method, and obtaining a reference to the `HttpSession` instance associated with the opening handshake from the `HandshakeRequest` object by calling

```
public Object getHttpSession()
```

Later in the chapter, you see an example of sharing data between web components and a WebSocket endpoint using this technique.

## HttpSession to WebSocket Session Association

Once the application has been running for a while, the association between the WebSocket `Session` instances and the `HttpSession` instance may not hold. If the `HttpSession` is terminated either by an explicit invalidation call or it times out, you cannot assume that the implementation will close any of the WebSocket `Sessions` started within that `HttpSession`. The situation in which the WebSocket implementation will in fact close WebSocket sessions associated with an `HttpSession` that terminates is when the user has authenticated with the web application and the WebSocket endpoints are protected by a security constraint. You do not want protected resources to remain active after the authenticated state that granted access to them has ended.

This means that if you want to make a stronger association between the `HttpSession` and WebSocket sessions that are initiated within it, you have some work to do.

Fortunately, the Servlet API gives you at least one way of doing it. A very useful property of `HttpSession` attributes, as described previously, is that they are removed from the `HttpSession` by the web container whenever the `HttpSession` ends, either through explicit invalidation or by timing out. As you can see in the listing that follows, if the object you add as an attribute implements the interface `HttpSessionBindingListener`, your object will be notified as it is being unbound from the `HttpSession`.

---

**Listing:**   *The javax.servlet.http.HttpSessionBindingListener*

```
public interface HttpSessionBindingListener {
    public void valueUnbound(HttpSessionBindingEvent hsbe);
    public void valueBound(HttpSessionBindingEvent hsbe);
}
```

In this way, you have the means by which to have a WebSocket endpoint instance notified when an `HttpSession` expires, giving it the chance to close its WebSocket connection and so keep a strong association between the `HttpSession` and the WebSocket `Session`.

## The HttpSession Sample

Let's take a look at this mechanism in action with the `HttpSession` sample. This is an application with a JavaScript client talking to a Java WebSocket server endpoint, wherein the Java WebSocket endpoint, the `EndpointWithHttpSession` class, manages a strong association between the WebSocket `Session` and the `HttpSession` by closing the WebSocket connection whenever the `HttpSession` terminates.

When you run the application, pressing a button on the web page will send a message to the server endpoint, initiating the WebSocket connection if necessary. Pressing another button will terminate the `HttpSession`. You can see from Figure 8-3 that the server endpoint instance knows the `HttpSession` that was in place when its WebSocket `Session` was established. And you can see that when the user invalidates the `HttpSession`, the WebSocket `Session` is closed.

The WebSocket endpoint `EndpointWithHttpSession` gains a reference to its `HttpSession` by means of the `HttpSessionConfigurator`, which inserts the `HttpSession` into the `ServerEndpointConfig` object's user properties by intercepting the opening handshake, and calling the

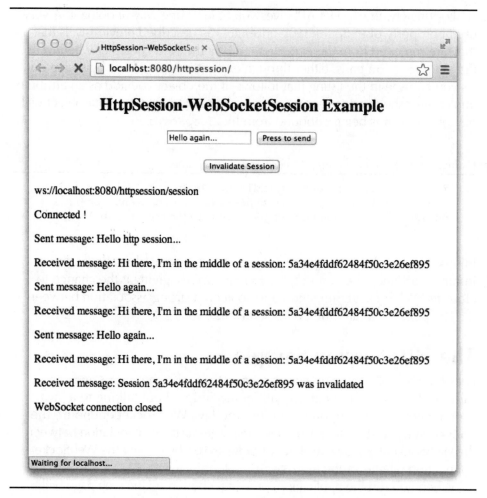

**FIGURE 8-3.** *Terminating the sessions*

`HandshakeRequest`'s `getHttpSession()` method. Let's look at what the `EndpointWithHttpSession` does with this `HttpSession` in its open event handling method:

**Listing:** *The EndpointWithHttpSession @OnOpen method*

```
@OnOpen
public void startConnection(Session session,
                    EndpointConfig config) {
```

```
        this.session = session;
        HttpSession httpSession =
                    (HttpSession) config.getUserProperties()
                            .get(HttpSessionConfigurator.HTTP_SESSION);
        HttpSessionInvalidationListener l =
                        new HttpSessionInvalidationListener(this);
        httpSession.setAttribute("httpsession-listener", l);
        httpSession.setMaxInactiveInterval(5);
    }
```

You can see that the method stores the reference to the WebSocket session in
an instance variable, and then retrieves the reference to the HttpSession
that this WebSocket instance is part of from the user properties on the
EndpointConfig object that was used to carry the reference by the
HttpSessionConfigurator. Next, the method creates a callback object,
the HttpSessionInvalidationListener, and adds it to the attributes on
the HttpSession. The HttpSessionInvalidationListener code in the
following listing simply calls back the EndpointWithSession when it is
unbound from the HttpSession.

**Listing:** *The HttpSessionInvalidationListener*

```
public class HttpSessionInvalidationListener
                        implements HttpSessionBindingListener {
    private EndpointWithHttpSession ewhs;

    public HttpSessionInvalidationListener(EndpointWithHttpSession es) {
        this.ewhs = es;
    }

    public void valueUnbound(HttpSessionBindingEvent hsbe) {
        ewhs.notifySessionUnboundMe(hsbe.getSession());
    }

    public void valueBound(HttpSessionBindingEvent hsbe) {}
}
```

Because this application never explicitly removes this attribute from the
HttpSession by calling the removeAttribute() method, the only
time it is removed from the HttpSession is when the HttpSession is
terminated.

The application contains a simple Java Servlet called the
InvalidateServlet, which you will see by browsing the source code and
which explicitly invalidates the HttpSession, thus causing a reload of the
web page to clear the output after a suitable delay.

**Listing:** *The InvalidateServlet Process Method*

```
protected void processRequest(HttpServletRequest request,
                             HttpServletResponse response)
                                  throws ServletException, IOException {
        request.getSession().invalidate();
        try {
            Thread.sleep(2000);
        } catch (Exception r) {}

        response.sendRedirect("index.jsp");
    }
```

This in turn invokes the `HttpSessionInvalidationListener`, which calls the `EndpointWithHttpSession` endpoint instance's `notifySessionUnboundMe()` method.

**Listing:** *The EndpointWithHttpSession Notification Handler Method*

```
public void notifySessionUnboundMe(HttpSession s) {
    try {
        this.session.getBasicRemote().sendText("Session " +
                            s.getId() + " was invalidated");
        this.session.close(
          new CloseReason(CloseReason.CloseCodes.NORMAL_CLOSURE,
                                    "HttpSession ended"));
    } catch (Exception r) {
        r.printStackTrace();
    }
}
```

As you can see in the code listing, this in turn sends the browser a message before closing the WebSocket connection and completing the strong association between the WebSocket connection and the `HttpSession` to which its opening handshake belonged.

If you play longer with this example application, you might notice that if the `HttpSession` times out, you will see the same message in the web page and the same closure of the WebSocket `Session`. `HttpSessions` are allowed to time out after their timeout interval, but the `HttpSession` object in the web container may not actually be invalidated as soon as the timeout interval is reached. However, if you wish to be sure of seeing the timeout effect, you can reload the web page after the original `HttpSession` has timed out to force a new `HttpSession` to be created, which will invalidate the old one and close the WebSocket connection.

Now that you have seen how to share application state specific to one user, it is a rather easy task to share application state common to all users. Simply use the `ServletContext` to do so. Obtaining a reference to the `ServletContext` is available on every `HttpSession` object using the

```
public ServletContext getServletContext()
```

method. So, for example, if you just need the `ServletContext` in a WebSocket endpoint in order to share application state with other web components (including other WebSockets, of course) in the same web application, and that is common to all users of the application, you could use a custom configurator such as the one shown in the listing that follows, to make it available on the `EndpointConfig` in your WebSocket endpoint.

**Listing:** *Using a Configurator to Get the ServletContext*

```
public class ServletContextConfigurator
                    extends ServerEndpointConfig.Configurator {
    public static String SERVLET_CONTEXT = "servlet-context";

    public void modifyHandshake(ServerEndpointConfig sec,
                HandshakeRequest request,
                HandshakeResponse response) {
        if (sec.getUserProperties().get(SERVLET_CONTEXT) != null) {
            ServletContext servletContext =
            ((HttpSession) request.getHttpSession()).getServletContext();
            sec.getUserProperties().put(SERVLET_CONTEXT, servletContext);
        }

    }

}
```

# Using EJBs from WebSocket Endpoints

When running in the Java EE platform, WebSocket server endpoints are *non-contextual managed beans*. This property means that the creation and destruction of the endpoint instances are managed by the Java EE platform, and also allows the EE platform to inject other Java EE components into your endpoint instances, if you so choose. These components can include Enterprise JavaBeans, database connections, or any other resource in the

JNDI namespace of the Java EE platform. There are many books and tutorials on the large topic of dependency injection in the Java EE platform, so we will restrict this short exploration to some of the most useful components: Enterprise JavaBeans.

In order to inject an EJB into a WebSocket endpoint, you first need to enable the dependency mechanism in the web application. You do this by adding a default `beans.xml` file to the `WEB-INF` directory of your web application, like this:

```
<?xml version="1.0" encoding="UTF-8"?>
<beans xmlns="http://java.sun.com/xml/ns/javaee"
       xmlns:xsi="http://www.w3.org/2001/XMLSchema-instance"
       xsi:schemaLocation="http://java.sun.com/xml/ns/javaee
               http://java.sun.com/xml/ns/javaee/beans_1_0.xsd">
</beans>
```

Once you have enabled dependency injection, you simply use the `@EJB` annotation to inject an EJB into your endpoint. The following code listing shows an endpoint that injects an EJB into itself.

**Listing:** *Simple EJB Injection*

```
import javax.ejb.EJB;

@ServerEndpoint("/my-endpoint")
public class MyEndpoint {
        @EJB
        private MyEJB myEJB;
...
}
```

Because the Java EE platform is responsible for creating the instance of the `MyEndpoint` class when a new client completes a successful opening handshake, it is able to inject a suitable instance of the `MyEJB` Enterprise JavaBean into the instance. This means that by the time the open handler method of the `MyEndpoint` class is called, the `myEJB` instance variable has already been initialized and is ready to take calls.

Two of the most useful types of EJBs to inject into a WebSocket endpoint are *stateful session beans* and *singleton* beans. If, in the preceding code listing, the `MyEJB` component is a stateful session bean, each time the new WebSocket endpoint is instantiated because a new client is connecting, the

Java EE platform will inject a new instance of the MyEJB component into the WebSocket endpoint. This makes this kind of bean useful to tie in with application state specific to a particular WebSocket connection. If, in the preceding code listing, the MyEJB component is a singleton bean, then each time the WebSocket endpoint is instantiated, the Java EE platform will inject the same instance of the MyEJB component into WebSocket endpoint instance. This makes injecting singleton EJBs into WebSocket endpoints a very useful way to share application state common to all connections to the application.

With this very simple introduction to two key use cases of how to bring EJBs into an application, let's take a look at a quick example.

# The EJB Example

In the following EJB example, we have a single server endpoint called EndpointWithEJBs.

**Listing:** *EndpointWithEJBs*

```
import javax.ejb.EJB;
import javax.websocket.OnError;
import javax.websocket.OnMessage;
import javax.websocket.server.ServerEndpoint;


@ServerEndpoint("/endpointwithejbs")
public class EndpointWithEJBs {
        @EJB
        private MyStatefulEJB myEJB;
        @EJB
        private MySingletonEJB mySingleton;

        @OnMessage
        public String hiThere(String message) {
            return "Hi. I have two EJBs: <br>  " + myEJB.getMessage() +
                                    "<br> " + mySingleton.getMessage();
        }

        @OnError
        public void error(Throwable t) {
            System.out.println("Error: " + t.getMessage());
        }

}
```

You can see that this is simply a variation on the Echo sample of Chapter 1, except that, in addition to responding to any incoming message, this server endpoint has two EJBs that it uses to formulate the message: a stateful session bean and a singleton. Using the @EJB annotation, the Java EE platform takes care of ensuring that these instance variable references to the EJBs are initialized correctly before the open handling method is called when a new client connects to the EndpointWithEJBs endpoint. Each EJB does the same thing: When it is first instantiated, it notes the current time. Whenever either EJB's getMessage() method is called, it returns a string containing the time it was created. This is a rough and ready way of being able to differentiate between different instances of the same bean by creation time.

When you make the first client connection to this EndpointWithEJBs, upon pressing the button on the web page, you might see output something like Figure 8-4, which shows you that the instances of the EJBs that the WebSocket endpoint is referencing were created at the same time. If, however, you reload the page, thereby causing a new WebSocket connection to be made to the WebSocket endpoint, you see something different when you press the button (see Figure 8-5).

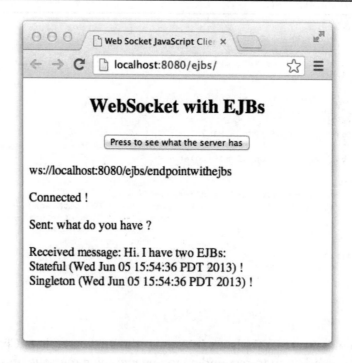

**FIGURE 8-4.** *EJB example on first connection*

**FIGURE 8-5.** *EJB example on later connection*

Notice this time that the singleton bean is saying it was created at the same time as when you made the first connection to the WebSocket endpoint. But this time, the stateful session bean referenced by the WebSocket endpoint is saying it was created at a different time.

This is a simple visual illustration of the fact that when you connected the second time to the WebSocket endpoint, the Java EE container created a second instance of the WebSocket endpoint to deal with the new connection. When it injected the EJBs into the second instance of the WebSocket endpoint, it used the same singleton bean as before because it is shared across all users, but it used a new instance of the stateful session bean, because this is a new connection.

**NOTE**
*Advanced developers can override the instance creation mechanism for WebSocket endpoints, and in so doing, lose the ability to automatically inject Java EE components such as EJBs into WebSocket endpoints so created.*

As you saw in Chapter 4, you can override the instance creation mechanism for server endpoints by creating a custom `ServerEndpointConfig.Configurator` class and overriding the following call:

```
public T getEndpointInstance(Class<T> c)
```

If you do not override this method, the Java EE platform creates the instances for you with all the injectability properties of managed beans.

You can manage your own instances of client endpoints simply by instantiating them yourself, and using either of the following methods on the `WebSocketContainer`, depending on what style of WebSocket endpoint you have:

```
Session connectToServer(Endpoint endpointInstance,
                                    ClientEndpointConfig cec,
                                                URI path)
Session connectToServer(Object annotatedEndpointInstance,
                                                URI path)
```

If you stick to the complementary `connectToServer()` methods that take the endpoint class instead of the instance,

```
Session connectToServer(Class<? extends Endpoint> endpointClass,
                                    ClientEndpointConfig cec,
                                                URI path)
Session connectToServer(Class<?> annotatedEndpointClass,
                                                URI path)
```

you will get the injectability properties of managed beans.

# The Chat Redux Example

Do you remember the Chat example way back in Chapter 4? As nice as it was, it was rather limited. For example, each time you refresh the web page, all the chat data is lost because the WebSockets on the page are closed when the browser forces a refresh. The same thing happens if you load a different page and then return to the chat page. In the Chat Redux application, we will apply some of the simple techniques you have learned in this chapter to store chat information in the `HttpSession`, and we will move the chat transcript code, which holds all the information about the group chat, into an EJB where it can be shared with a number of Java Servlets.

Before you look at the code, let's take a quick look at how the application has changed from the user's perspective.

When you first sign in, you will see that there are some new elements in the main page (Figure 8-6). Notice that toward the bottom of the page, the username is displayed in the HTML, and there is a link to find out more about the chat data. Following the link takes you to a breakdown of the chat data into various forms (Figure 8-7). Notice again that the HTML of the page has remembered your username from the chat session on the previous page. Meanwhile, if you were logged in as another participant when you moved to this page, a new message was generated when you left the page (Figure 8-8), saying that you stepped out of the room for a minute. Upon your return to the main chat page,

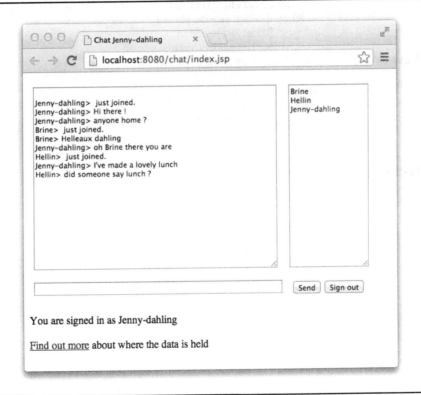

**FIGURE 8-6.** *Chat main window*

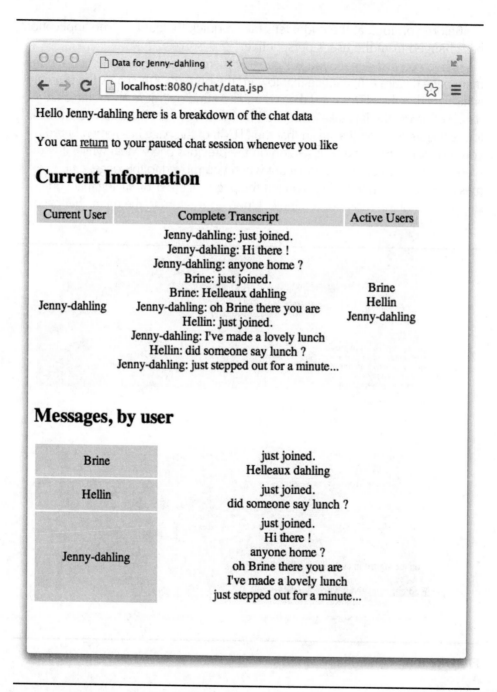

**FIGURE 8-7.** *Chat data window*

**FIGURE 8-8.** *Chat main window, while you were away*

you will notice that all the chat session data has been "remembered," and in addition, everyone is told that you have returned (Figure 8-9).

Let's take a look at the main elements of this application and its main interactions. The chat conversation is managed between a JavaScript client in the index.jsp page and the ChatServer endpoint. The index.jsp additionally uses a jsp:include to bring in the output of servlet NameServlet, which simply sends the name of the currently active user of the chat application. The username is readily available to that servlet because it is available in

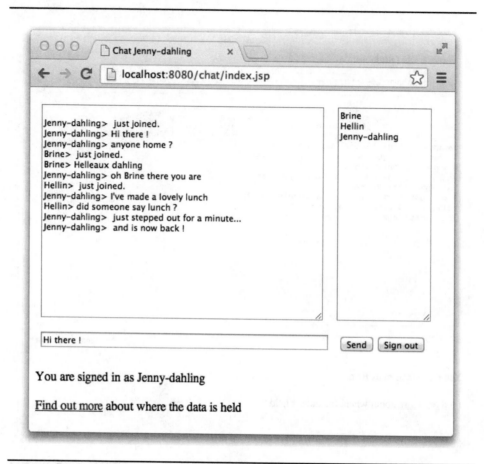

**FIGURE 8-9.** *Chat main window, back again*

the `HttpSession`. The following listing shows the main method of the
`NameServlet` code.

**Listing:** *NameServlet Process Method*

```
protected void processRequest(HttpServletRequest request,
                              HttpServletResponse response)
                    throws ServletException, IOException {
    response.setContentType("text/html;charset=UTF-8");
    PrintWriter out = response.getWriter();
```

```
    try {
        HttpSession session = request.getSession();
        String username =
                (String) session.getAttribute(ChatServer.USERNAME_KEY);
        out.println(username);
    } finally {}
}
```

The username is placed in the HttpSession when the ChatServer processes a new user request, as you can see in this excerpt from the ChatServer endpoint code.

**Listing:**   *ChatServer Processing a New User*

```
void processNewUser(NewUserMessage message) {
    String newUsername = this.validateUsername(message.getUsername());
    this.confirmUser(newUsername);
    this.registerUser(newUsername);
    this.broadcastUserListUpdate();
    this.sendTranscript();
    this.addMessage(" just joined.");
}
...
private void registerUser(String username) {
    this.httpSession.setAttribute(USERNAME_KEY, username);
    this.updateUserList();
}
```

The ChatServer uses the TranscriptBean to store the chat transcript and maintain the current active user list. The TranscriptBean is marked with the @Singleton annotation, so there is a single instance of this EJB per application. This means that all the ChatServer instances share the same TranscriptBean instance, and so everyone is reading and writing to the same transcript. This is also the same application-global instance of the transcript used by the servlets that power the data.jsp page in order to produce the data output on the page. These servlets are the TranscriptServlet, UsernamesServlet, and UserMessagesServlet, and they all use the following declaration:

```
@javax.ejb.EJB
private TranscriptBean transcriptBean;
```

and rely on the Java EE platform to initialize the reference correctly. The ChatServer uses the configurator technique, ChatServerConfigurator, you learned earlier to obtain a reference to the HttpSession and store it in EndpointConfig.

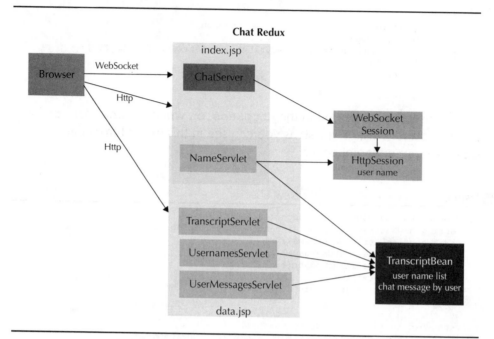

**FIGURE 8-10.** *Chat Redux Architecture*

You can see clearly in the following diagram (Figure 8-10) the main components of this chat application where the key pieces of application information are held.

We leave you to explore the code in more detail to see exactly where the associations are set up, and we leave you the exercise of closing the chat session when the HttpSession times out.

# Summary

In this chapter, we have started an exploration of how to expand the scope of a WebSocket server endpoint by integrating with other Java EE components in the Java EE platform. We looked at how to associate the current WebSocket endpoint with an HttpSession and locate the ServletContext of the containing web container, and explored the possibilities of sharing user state and global application state with other web components in the web container. We started an exploration of how to inject other Java EE components such as EJBs into WebSocket server endpoints in order to use preexisting middleware EJB components, and take advantage of the other services readily available to EJB components such as transactions and database connectivity.

Finally, we took the Chat application from Chapter 4 and made it HttpSession-aware, allowing it to share its state with a singleton EJB and web components that presented a report on the current state of play in the chat room, and in order to enable the chat session to be replicated even when the user navigates to another page and returns at a later time to the chat page.

We hope that this has whet your appetite to do much more exploration with Java WebSockets and other web and Java EE components to build modern, engaging, and powerful web applications!

# Index

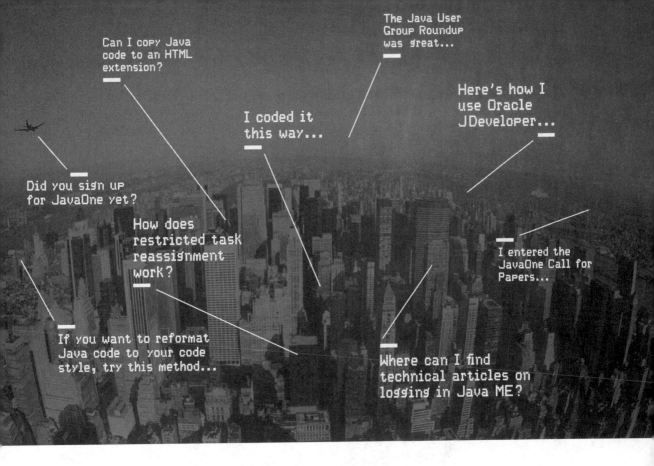

# Oracle Technology Network. It's code for sharing expertise.

Come to the best place to collaborate with other IT professionals on everything Java.

Oracle Technology Network is the world's largest community of developers, administrators, and architects using Java and other industry-standard technologies with Oracle products.

Sign up for a free membership and you'll have access to:

- Discussion forums and hands-on labs
- Free downloadable software and sample code
- Product documentation
- Member-contributed content

Take advantage of our global network of knowledge.

JOIN TODAY ▷ Go to: oracle.com/technetwork/java

## Reach More than 700,000 Oracle Customers with Oracle Publishing Group

### Connect with the Audience that Matters Most to Your Business

**Oracle Magazine**
The Largest IT Publication in the World
Circulation: 550,000
Audience: IT Managers, DBAs, Programmers, and Developers

**Profit**
Business Insight for Enterprise-Class Business Leaders to Help Them Build a Better Business Using Oracle Technology
Circulation: 100,000
Audience: Top Executives and Line of Business Managers

**Java Magazine**
The Essential Source on Java Technology, the Java Programming Language, and Java-Based Applications
Circulation: 125,000 and Growing Steady
Audience: Corporate and Independent Java Developers, Programmers, and Architects

For more information or to sign up for a FREE subscription:
Scan the QR code to visit Oracle Publishing online.